Louisa M Macomber

An autumnal wreath

a religious souvenir

Louisa M Macomber

An autumnal wreath
a religious souvenir

ISBN/EAN: 9783337374143

Printed in Europe, USA, Canada, Australia, Japan

Cover: Foto ©Lupo / pixelio.de

More available books at **www.hansebooks.com**

A RELIGIOUS SOUVENIR.

BY MRS. LOUISA M. MACOMBER.

HYDE PARK:
PRINTED AT THE OFFICE OF THE NORFOLK COUNTY GAZETTE.
1871.

Entered according to Act of Congress, in the year 1871, by
MRS. LOUISA M. MACOMBER,
In the office of the Librarian of Congress, at Washington, D. C.

INTRODUCTION.

These leaves, which have been gathered at long intervals, and many of them lain away in dusty drawers since the writer's early girlhood, are now, at the solicitation of friends, collected and woven into a wreath, to be presented as a keepsake to our many friends. Some of them have appeared in print, yet but very few of them have ever been suffered to see the light. Very many of them were gathered in hope and gladness, when the rich blessings of health and strength were ours to enjoy; when the inspiring voice of friendship was music to our ear, and when we ever delighted to reciprocate those tender and endearing sentiments; others were gathered from the dark boughs of the mournful cypress, when the heart was oppressed with its load of grief, when the kind ministrations of friendship were as a soothing balm to the wounded spirit; while many, indeed, were gathered from beneath the drooping branches of the weeping willow, where love and friendship have long since reposed in dust.

The writer makes no pretensions to erudition in the production of this simple wreath; the sentiments of which it is composed are the spontaneous outgushings of a heart whose sincerity and simplicity must be its only apology. Coming as it does, slightly touched by the hoar frost of life's early winter, it may, perhaps, be found devoid of both beauty and fragrance, unless the sunshine of indulgence and the sweet dew of friendship shall gently descend upon its leaves.

Very much do we regret that we have been compelled to defer from year to year the publication of these pages, in the vain hope that improved health might sometime enable us to bestow greater attention to their revision and arrangement than we have been able to do.

Some of the pieces may not, we fear, be perfectly satisfactory to some of our friends who may not be in sympathy with our religious sentiments. We feel very desirous, even ambitious, of pleasing every one of our valued friends; yet we so love the doctrine of the Universal Fatherhood of God, the Brotherhood of Man, and the ultimate holiness and happiness of all our race, that we feel impelled to avow it, even here; but yet, we would ever cherish the broadest charity for *all*.

Perhaps some of our Catholic friends may take exception at what we have expressed of Pius IX. To all such we would say, that it is not the *religion* of the Pope to which we object, but to his bitter hostility to the dissemination of knowledge, and to every form of popular government, his arbitrary assumption of temporal power, and his impious pretensions to a prerogative or attribute which belongs only to the Supreme Being.

Realizing as we do that this humble offering is intended only for the eye of friendship, and is not to go beyond the charmed circle of relatives and friends, yet we feel a painful diffidence, even at that; and still we can but cherish the pleasing hope that, with all its imperfections, it may prove an acceptable souvenir,

— a kind of keepsake, sacred to friendship, and consecrated to the memory of departed days, very long after the heart which dictated and the hand that wrote it shall have mingled with their native elements.

L. M. M.

CONTENTS.

	PAGE
Dedicatory,	11
The Fiat,	14
The Messiah's Advent,	15
Whom Having not Seen, We Love,	18
The Eucharist,	22
Aspirations,	25
Life,	28
Soul-Thoughts,	29
Morning,	31
The Veiled Heart,	33
Truth,	36
Be Glad, My Heart,	37
My First Schoolmaster,	39
Lines Written on Seeing the Picture of a Mad Woman in Chains,	44
An Apostrophe to Time,	47
A Wish,	49
Summer Friends,	51
Fain would I Fly Away and be at Rest,	52
The Heart,	53
Foot-prints,	56
The Morning Stars Sang Together,	58
Memory,	60
The Ghost of Unrest,	61
Lines on a Centenarian Woman,	63
Pre-existence,	67

CONTENTS.

	PAGE
The Parting Hour,	71
Alone,	74
To My Mother, on My Marriage,	78
To an Old Schoolmate,	80
To One in Heaven,	83
Come Up Higher,	85
Love Without Alloy,	86
Kindred Souls,	89
The Fatherland,	91
Friendship,	93
Lost Jewels,	95
My Angel Watcher,	99
Mother Love,	101
Our Mother,	102
May,	105
Though Sorrow Endure for a Night, yet Joy Cometh in the Morning,	107
The Old Carpet,	110
Our Home,	113
Lines Written on Returning from a Journey,	116
Our Garden,	118
Flowers,	122
The Black Cricket,	124
To a Stuffed Duck,	126
A Talk with a Blue Violet by Moonlight,	129
Summer Eve,	131
The Sunset Hour,	133
Sunshine,	135
To a Red-breast, Singing,	137
The Mysterious Bird,	139
The Wounded Bird,	142
To a Friend, on Being Presented with a Beautiful Tea Rose,	144
On Visiting Drew Brook,	145
A Song — The Beautiful Trees,	148
My Brother,	151
The Widowed Heart,	154

CONTENTS.

	PAGE
The Last Day of Summer,	157
Closet Prayer,	160
To My Husband, on New Year's Day,	162
To Lavinia,	163
To Octavia,	166
To Carrie,	168
Lines,	170
Hope,	171
To One Beloved,	173
A Song — The Hermit,	176
To the Great Sea,	179
The Drought,	184
To L——e, suggested by Reading one of his Poems,	188
The Resurrected Harp,	192
Unwritten Music,	195
In War Time,	199
Death of Our Martyred President,	202
The Slave Mother's Lament,	206
The Death of Lincoln,	210
An Emblem,	112
Call me Not Back,	213
To the Oriole,	216
In Affliction,	218
The Good Shepherd,	221
In Memoriam,	223
Lines suggested by seeing a picture of our Immortal Washington placing the Victor-Wreath upon the head of our Martyred Lincoln,	226
What Ye Know not Now, Ye Shall Know Hereafter,	229
My Mother's Grave,	232
The True Friend,	234
My Father's Bible,	236
My Father's Burial Hour,	239
The Dearest Name,	242
Jesus Wept,	244
Hour of Communion,	247

CONTENTS.

	PAGE
My All, My All!	249
Trust in God,	253
The Good Old Pilgrim,	254
Intemperance,	256
To Pius IX.,	259
The Present Epoch,	264
Garibaldi,	267
Impromptu,	270
The Last Decade,	271
The Place of Judgment,	273
The Winged Hours,	285
He is Not Here,	288
Compensation,	293
The Autumn of Life,	295
October of Life,	297
Husband,	300
Birthday Reflections,	302
In Sickness,	304
Lines on the Death of Alice Cary	308
Lights and Shadows,	311
Immortality,	314
What is Death?—There is No Death,	317
Flesh and Spirit,	319
Hour of Anguish,	321
Hope,	322
Our Father Who Art in Heaven,	323
His Tender Mercies are over all the Works of His Hands,	325
Sympathy,	327
Hope in Affliction,	329
Hereafter,	330
Thoughts of Heaven,	334
Who Will Wind the Clock?	337
On Seeing God,	340
To Death,	343
Done with Earth,	344

DEDICATORY.

I dedicate to you, dear friends,
   This simple wreath of autumn leaves;
An humble offering 'tis indeed,
   Which love inspires and friendship weaves.

"Smit with the love of sacred song,"
   With truth and beauty's potent power,
I give what is so dear to me;
   Friends, will ye accept the dower?

Tho' late in life I twine this wreath,
   I trust it may acceptance find;
Since the sweet flowers which bloomed in youth
   Have left their fragrance on my mind.

Their fragrance, but their bloom is gone,
   And where birds sang on every spray,
Are withered leaves without the flowers,
   But hope triumphing o'er decay.

As the autumnal sunset's glow
   Doth deepen as the days decline,

So does the love within my soul
   Grow deeper for those friends of mine.

The loved, the tried of early years,
   Who walked with me life's pleasant ways,
The valued few who yet remain
   To cheer my autumn days.

Many who have walked with us,
   Keeping faithful watch and ward,
Have lain aside their pilgrim staff,
   And gone to their reward.

And some of us who sowed in hope
   Have reaped in bitter tears;
While some have garnered precious sheaves,
   The fruit of patient years.

I would a worthier gift were mine,
   One worthy of your care and trust;
Whose bloom and fragrance might survive
   When I am in the dust.

Poor as it is, its every leaf
   Betokens kind, sincere regard;
And if it does acceptance find,
   'Twill be to me a rich reward.

Perhaps as you may scan it o'er,
   It may revive some pleasing thought;

Awake the memory of loved scenes,
  Which hope and fancy wrought.

Recall the vanished hours again,
  Revive the memory of the dead,
Who with sandals wet with early dew,
  Life's morning paths with us did tread.

Cheering to me as heaven's own light,
  And sweeter than spring violet's breath,
Is the sweet faith I cherish yet,
  That love surviveth death.

THE FIAT.

"He spake and it was done; He commanded and it stood fast."

A voice went forth; profoundest depths were stirred,
Darkness retired at that Omnific word;
Chaos, obedient, vanished from the scene,
And lo! a world stood forth, calm and serene.
Yon brilliant sun careering through mid-heaven,
Night's glorious orbs, the moon and stars, were given
To light the temple where our God presides
Amidst His glories, yet His presence hides.

Oh! the stern grandeur of that temple, where
The thunder organ peals amid the lightning's glare!
Would that each heart an altar might become,
Where incense offered to that Holy One
Might rise upon the winds, whose voice proclaims
The august wonders of His glorious name:
Might mingle with the surging, loud-voiced flood,
And swell the chorus, "Thou, O God, art good."

THE MESSIAH'S ADVENT.

A purer air breathes o'er Judea's hills,
A holier calm the soul of Nature fills;
Retiring day, far in the rosy west,
Proclaims the dawn of promised blessedness.

The balmy air now gently doth distil
A kindlier dew than e'er on Herman fell;
The distant hills are tipped with mellow light
Of Rising Cynthia—Empress of the night.

The tranquil shepherds with their flocks recline;
Meek innocents—emblems of the Divine!
The Lamb of God who takes our sins away—
The heavenly Shiloh of the Prophet-lay.

Why is the blood-stained weapon in its sheath?
Why round the nation's brow the Olive-wreath?
*Why that high, massive dome with gorgeous walls,
Its portals closed and silence in its halls?

Why from the heart does hoary error groan?
The Idol-god, why tottering on his throne?

*Temple of Janus.

As darkness flies before the god of day,
So do the types and shadows pass away.

Why baleful war,—that scourge of ages past—
With blood-stained laurels, withering, stand aghast?
His marshall'd hosts have left the sanguine plain,—
No hostile navies sweep the heaving main.

Yon orient star high o'er the mountains shine;
What means the stranger—favored Palestine?
Bright beauteous star—mild, pensive, and serene,
Precursor of the lovely Nazarine!

On, on it moves majestic up the sky,
Bright with the radiance of Eternity;
It leads the inquiring wanderers from afar
To worship Him, the bright, the morning star!

The Prince of Peace approaches!—O how sweet
To lay the heart's pure offerings at his feet!
To yield the soul's devotion and its praise
To Him, who comes, the Saviour of our race!

What means that strain of music, soft and low?
Jordan has caught the sound, and in its flow
Echoes it back to Zion's sacred towers,
Through hallowed groves and consecrated bowers.

Is it the warbling of some Prophet-lyre,
Baptized anew with heaven's own altar-fire?
Or does some Eden-strain delight the ear,
Which thrilled the heart e'er earth had known a tear?

Oh, how it fires the bosom! Look on high!
'Tis not of Earth—'tis heaven's own minstrelsy!
It's drapery's drawn aside—behold they come!
The angel-host warm from the spirit-home.

They near the earth—how glorious they appear!
List! 'tis for man they leave their native sphere.
"Good will to man!" the burden of their song,
Dissolves the heart in bliss as 't flows along.

"Good will to man!" each shining seraph cries,
"Good will to man!" heaven's echoing dome replies,
The earth repeated—and the bounding main—
"Good will to man!" then earth was mute again.

High heaven then paused, the wondrous work to
    scan;
No angel-mind could sound redemption's plan,
When boundless love, that mystery undefined,
Gave to the world the Saviour of mankind.

"WHOM, HAVING NOT SEEN, WE LOVE."

I have not seen that pitying face,
    Which once was bathed in blood-like sweat;
Nor seen those meekly-flowing locks,
    Which oft were with the night-dews wet.

Yet contemplation loves to range
    Those paths thy sacred feet have prest;
A lowly, meek sojourner then,—
    Thou had'st not where thine head to rest.

Oft, ere morn's dewy twilight hour,
    When Nature lay in sweet repose,
Amidst the mountain solitude
    Thy meekly pleading voice arose.

Before the silent stars went out,
    Or the pale moon sank in the west,
Thou sought'st thy heavenly Father's face,
    And laid thy cares upon his breast.

How warms my heart, while fancy scans
    Thy works of love in Gallilee?

Or where the Kedron gently flows,
    Or murmurs the Tiberian sea.

Or where the Jordan's cooling waves
    Unto the sacred rite were given;
And where the mystic dove came down,
    Proclaiming *Thee a Son of Heaven*.

I have not seen thee on the wave,
    When all was terror and alarm;
When the sweet accents of thy voice
    Moved o'er the deep and all was calm.

In melting strains, Jerusalem,
    Flowed the soft cadence of that voice;
Thy sick, thy lame, thy blind among,
    While angels, bending low, rejoiced.

When Death, unwont to yield his dead,
    Felt thy firm grasp his vitals wound,
And Lazarus from the grave came forth
    In death's pale drapery, closely bound.

I have not heard that deep-drawn sigh,
    That sigh which rent thy sorrowing breast,
When thou, in dark Gethsemane, knelt
    With a world's weight of woe opprest.

I have not seen thee, toiling, bear
    Thy heavy cross up Calvary's height,
Nor seen thee on that cross expire,
    When the pale sun refused the sight.

Nor have I heard that melting prayer,
    That prayer which moved the ear of heaven;
That those who thirsted for thy blood
    Might, through thy blood, be all forgiven.

I have not heard the low lament,
    The agony of grief profound,
The soul's deep prayer, the stifled sigh,
    Of Salem's daughter's weeping round.

Nor have I seen, with aching heart,
    Thy sacred head in death reclined,
The heaving of the expiring breast,
    The struggling of the God-like mind.

When resurrection poured its light
    Within that dark and gloomy grot,
And Thou, with angel-bands, came forth,
    With rapturous joy, I saw thee not.

Yet, 'tho my pensive fancy roves
    Among thy hills, O Palestine!
And listen to each mournful breeze,
    It cannot catch that voice divine.

And 'tho I have not heard thy voice,
   Nor seen thy face, thy hands, thy side;
And 'tho my feet may never press
   The mountain top where thou hast died,

Yet, Faith, midst angel-bands, beholds
   That form—to bless with arms spread wide,
Where cherubim and seraphim
   Fall down to adore the Crucified.

My raptured soul, o'erpowered with love,
   Bows lowly down—would kiss thy feet—
With grateful heart adore thy grace,
   And, patient, wait thy face to meet.

Deep in my heart of hearts enshrined,
   Thy name shall live, divinely sweet,
'Tho every earthly tie expires,
   And cold in death it cease to beat.

THE EUCHARIST.

"For as oft as ye do this, do it in remembrance of me."

Remember thee, thou Son of God,
Thou who alone the winepress trod?
Tho' earthly friends be all forgot,
Jesus, thy friends forget thee not.

Remember thee?—Jesus, we feel
It is our highest bliss to kneel
Within thy sacred courts, and here
Commemorate thy love so dear.

Remember thee?—the Truth, the Way?
Thy love, dear Lord, to us convey,
While turns to thee each wishful eye,
And throbs the heart with thee so nigh.

Remember thee?—can we forget
The hopes which cheer our spirits yet,
To see thy face, thy hands, thy side,
O Lamb of God, the Crucified?

Remember thee?—Earth's holiest morn
Was when the promised Christ was born;
Divinest gift of heaven to man;
With grateful hearts the gift we scan.

Remember thee?—thy works of love
Our very inmost soul doth move,
We see thee raise the fainting head,
We see thee bring to life the dead.

Remember thee?—we hear thee pray
On the dark mount, ere break of day;
We hear thee raise the sacred song,
We see thee feed the famished throng.

Remember thee?—we almost hear
The dashing waves, so cold and drear,
When thou, on that frail vessel, stood
With all the grandeurs of a God.

We hear those accents, "Peace be still,"
The storm-cloud, dark, obeys thy will,
The awful waves retire and sleep
On the calm bosom of the deep.

Remember thee?—we see thee stand
With pleading voice, and outstretched hand,

Presiding at the sacred feast,
Inviting all to be thy guest.

Remember thee?—oft turns our eye
To that sad mount where thou didst die;
Hopes cluster round that hallowed cross,
Compared with which all else is dross.

Remember thee?—we call to mind
The rock-bound tomb, where thou, enshrined,
Didst sleep, didst rise, and bring to view
A life which angels never knew.

Remember thee?—we'll ne'er forget
When thou didst stand on Olivet;
The last adieu, that tender word,
We love thee our ascended Lord.

And when life's closing hour shall come,
And heaven remands our spirits home,
Sweet to the soul will be the thought,
Jesus, that thou'lt forget us not.

ASPIRATIONS.

High over head, on sapphire plains,
   Where camp the ancient stars at night,
Eager I turn the inquiring gaze,
   And plead for light — more light.

I search for light — diviner light;
   My eyes forever more
Essay to pierce the mystic veil
   Of that eternal door,

Which he on Patmos' Isle looked through,
   While robed in vestments of decay;
The glory of whose faintest gleam
   Would pale to death earth's brightest day.

I thirst, I ever, ever thirst,
   And nought will quench this flame,
Until the dust goes back to dust,
   And soul returns from whence it came.

I thirst for knowledge, wisdom, light,
   A beauty which is undefined.

A vision of extatic bliss
   Deep in my inmost soul is shrined.

Spirit of mine, drink deep
   At life's immortal founts;
Drink deep from wisdom's flowing stream,
   There bathe thy wings and mount.

Where prophet-bards have swept the lyre,
   And bathed in heaven's own light, —
But stop not there, O stop not there,
   Still upward wing thy flight.

High, higher, higher,
   Is deeply graven on my heart,—
Written as with a pen of fire
   Upon its inmost part.

A voice forever in my ear
   Calls with a high behest,
O come up higher, higher, higher,
   Nor there attempt to rest.

But upward, onward, evermore,
   Toward the soul's eternal source;
Aspiring ever to explore,
   Still upward urge thy course.

Thou hast not, Father, made the soul
    To famish with intense desire;
The spirit's depths thou dost pervade;
    To thee, to thee, it must aspire.

Nothing but thine infinity
    The restless, thirsting soul can fill,
Its deathless, yearning, deep desire
    For something better still.

LIFE.

Serene the spirit's dawn;
   How calm it doth begin;
Like a pale star of morn,
   Unstained, unscathed by sin,
A spark struck off from Deity
And destined for eternity.

A path before it lies,
   Hours, days, and months, and years,
With here a sunny mount,
   And there a vale of tears;
Its destiny it must fulfill,
A power unseen directs its will.

SOUL-THOUGHTS.

I have no righteousness to plead,
   Yet, Lord, I love thy sacred name;
I love thee; why should I not?
   My spirit from thy bosom came,

And shall soar back to thee again,
   When dust returns to silent dust;
Shall glow an ever-brightening flame,
   In hope and love and trust.

I joy to think a time will come
   When every child of Adam's race
Within thy temple, broad and vast,
   Will find a dwelling-place.

In joyful hope I wait the day,
   The restitution of all things;
I joy to see the time pass by,
   Which the grand consummation brings.

A whole eternity of life
   Spreads out before my sight,
And thought, o'erwhelmed at the vast scene,
   Flies to the Infinite.

I grasp the pillars of his throne,
   And death's grim powers defy;
Safe, held by my own Father's hand,
   How can I fear to die?

MORNING.

'Tis morn! midst roses newly blown,
　Whose fragrant incense breathe to heaven,
Father, I'd kneel beneath thy throne,
　And offer praise for mercies given.

Accept, dear God, through thine own Son,
　My praise for blessings ever new;
I've nothing but a grateful heart,—
　Will thou accept the offering due?

When yesternight its lights put out,
　And yonder sun had sunk to bed,
With night's dark curtains round about,
　Thine angels hovered o'er my head.

As thou did walk amidst the flowers,
　In dewy Eden's sinless prime,
Thou walkest now at early hours,
　And wak'st the morning's chime.

I love to see thee through thy works,
  When curious buds and flowers expand,
And humbly hold such sacred talks
  About thy plastic hand.

Nature, sweet medium drawn between,
  As friend with friend, now face to face
I can address thy presence, e'en
  No Eden-sword doth guard the place.

THE VEILED HEART.

"Nevertheless, when it shall turn to the Lord, the veil shall be taken away."

I saw an eye that could not weep,
  The fountain-head of tears had dried,
The tender chords, which grief did sweep,
  Long since had withered up and died.

And Oh! that heart of finest mould,
  Deep wounded, scathed by error's tone—
I saw that heart laid bare—'twas cold—
  Pulseless as monumental stone;

And on its tablet I beheld,
  Deep graven as with living fire,
Some souls, obnoxious to their God,
  Were doomed to his eternal ire.

And o'er that heart a veil was flung,
  Black as the darkness of the night;
I turned aside, my heart was wrung,
  To see that sad, untimely blight.

No light throughout its chambers shone,
    Save one, like comet's baleful glare,
Presaging darkness, death, and gloom,
    Till martyred hope was buried there.

I cried, "Is there no balm in Gilead,—
    No antidote against despair,—
Is there no arm that's strong to save,—
    No holy, healing, unction there?"

A pause ensued; 'twas solemn, deep,
    Profound, as was that one in heaven
Before that thunder-tempest broke,
    Or ere that seventh seal was riven.

And then a beauteous form appeared,
    Pure, radiant, as that seraph bright
Which woke to song the morning stars,
    When God first said, "Let there be light."

Like Pity, bending o'er the tomb,
    Where death itself can do no more,
She meekly bent her radiant form,
    And poured the balm of healing o'er.

Then, Phœnix-like, it lived again,
    From the dark dust of death arose,
I heard the sweet-toned anthem peal
    A requiem o'er departed woes.

An altar then that heart beseemed,
 I saw the smoke of incense rise,
I saw it pierce the depths of heaven,
 A pure, accepted sacrifice.

Earth still has hearts as sorely crushed,—
 How views such scenes the Omniscient eye?
From gilded domes, where Moloch reigns,
 Ascends to heaven the burning sigh!

And shall this Hydra always reign?
 Hail! watchman, hail! "What of the night?"
The morning breaks, the shadows flee—
 Hear ye that voice? "I am the light!"

Go tell that form of dark despair
 That the last tear shall soon be wept,
And the dark veil, which he has spread
 O'er human hearts, will soon be swept.

TRUTH.

One spirit pure, with white wing undefiled,
    Lowly and meek as violet of the sod,
Still walks our earth, often in sackcloth clad,
    And yet majestic as a very god.

Out of great tribulation she hath come,
    The blood of martyrs still upon her hem,
Mingling with hers, drawn from the inner heart,
    While she the fight of faith hath fought for them.

Thine offspring, thine is she, Eternal God,
    Cherished by thee and heaven's immortal breath;
'Tho crushed to earth she soon will rise again,
    For she can never taste the pangs of death.

Once pierced and nailed to Calvary's mournful cross,
    The awful hour when mercy veiled the sun,
Hers was the triumph,—thine be all the praise!
    The world's eternal gain that day was won.

BE GLAD, MY HEART.

No more, no more, my mournful lyre,
    Attune thy notes to sadness;
Invoke the muse of cheerful lay,
    And sing one song of gladness.

Earth has its merry-making things,
    And all the air's alive with song;
Thou say'st thou'd sing wert thou a bird,—
    Pray to what tribe would'st thou belong?

All creatures have their sunless day,
    And all their starless night;
Thou coulds't not know the night from day,
    If both alike were light.

And had'st thou never known a grief,
    Nor ever felt a pain,
Nevermore would'st thou aspire
    A higher bliss to gain.

Then drink thy cup of bitter-sweet,
 Nor murmuring turn away;
'Twas mingled by a Father's hand—
 He cares for thee alway.

MY FIRST SCHOOLMASTER.

My first, my good, old teacher,
   I never have forgot:
He was in the "sere and yellow leaf,"
   When I was a little tot.

Just let me tell you how he looked,—
   My teacher of the olden time,—
Before I'd learned my a b c,
   Or ever thought of rhyme.

I see him, as before me now,—
   He was straight, and tall, and slim;
And tho' many things I have forgot,
   I well remember him.

His forehead,—it was broad and high,
   His nose was rather aquiline,
His face was ruddy, oval, fair,
   And his mouth was very fine.

His eyes beamed with intelligence,
   Were bright, and mild, and blue,

And the pale pink color of his head
   'Midst his thin locks shone through.

The years his hair had whitened,
   And his eyes were getting dim;
But the golden spectacles he wore
   So well befitted him

That he seldom made a blunder,
   Owing to imperfect sight;
And all our good old master did
   We ever thought was right.

He was somewhat antiquated—
   He loved the things of old;
So to quite ancient costumes
   He tenaciously did hold.

He wore those fashioned breeches
   Which came just to his knees;
They were like those in pictures
   Which one quite often sees.

And he sported silver buckles
   On his knees, one on each shoe;
And the stockings which he wore
   Were silken, and were blue.

His vest was a pale buff,
   Which reached exceeding low,

To meet the breeches which he wore,
  In the long time ago.

A snow-white kerchief round his neck,
  My teacher always wore;
'Twas folded very neat and broad—
  Three inches—perhaps four.

He wore a gown, oh! such a gown
  We then had never seen,
'Twas of the colors of the rainbow,
  An yet was mostly green.

His cane was polished hickory,
  Given him, when a boy,
By a kind old Indian sachem,
  Whose name was Wickaroy.

He was a worthy bachelor,
  Fast wedded to his school;
And so kind he ever ruled us,
  That he did not seem to rule.

Rough men styled him the "sucking dove,"
  He was so meek in all his ways;
For there were bad, as well as good,
  In my childhood days.

His manners, of the olden school,
  Were gentle and refined,

Formed in those days when it was thought
  To be polite was to be kind.

He neither drank, nor smoked, nor chewed—
  He was a temperate man;
And as a theologian,
  He stood in the front van.

His piety was simple,
  Yet his creed was most severe;
He taught that to the heart of God
  None but the elect were dear.

All about these Godly mysteries,
  He fain would have us know;
I remember once I answered him,
  "If I was God, I'd not do so."

In our rural district, then,
  Hotels did not abound,
And so our worthy teacher
  Was compelled to " board around."

Children were thick as blackberries,
  And our dwelling seemed alive
With little responsibilities,
  A literal human hive.

We would flock around his easy chair,
  And chatter, and chirp, and sing,

Like a flock of new-fledged birds,
  In time of early spring.

Sometimes we brought him flowers,
  And sometimes berries, red;
While pleased he'd smile and answer
  Every word he said.

He carried a green umbrella
  To school, and 'twas such fun
To get within its shadow,
  And screen us from the sun.

Oh! blessed days, how swift they pass'd,
  Their memory still is sweet;
Oh! for one hour, again to sit,
  A simple child, low at his feet.

LINES

Written on seeing the picture of a mad woman, in chains

Thou child of fearful destiny,
   Strange fire is in thine eye,
Which burns with a consuming heat,
   Parching life's fountain dry.

I gaze into thy fierce, red eyes,
   And scan their depths of jet;
With pity, more than tongue can tell—
   Thou art my sister yet!

Oh, could I read thy life's sad page,
   The cause—the anguish of thy mind—
Yet, 'tis enough for me to know
   Thou art of human kind.

I weep for thy sorrowing heart
   As I gaze on thy noble brow,
But more deeply I grieve for that intellect
   Which lies in ruins now.

The priest of the inner temple's fled;
   The reasoning god has left his throne,
And thou art raving in the dark—
   Imprisoned—chained—alone!

There is dust upon thine head,
   But no tear is in thine eye,
And thine unshod feet in galling chains
   Are burning—hot and dry.

And there's blood upon thy robes,
   And on thy relentless chain—
'Tis the generous blood from thy bursting heart,
   Which comes to relieve thy pain.

Oh for the healing dew—
   For that tender, soothing rain,
Which heals the heart's deep, festering wounds,
   And cools the burning brain.

Oh for the word which broke
   From pitying lips of yore;
To calm and soothe thy frenzied mind,
   Thy reason's light restore.

Oh for the music-breathing strains
   Which swept the prophet's lyre,
Which calmed the maddened monarch's soul,
   And quenched its raging fire.

Ah, how my being's depths are stirred,
  As I see the passers-by
Glance at thy pale and haggard face
  With an unpitying eye.

We'll tell it not in modern times,
  That in the years gone by,
The frenzied woman, bound in chains,
  Was left alone to die.

Thank God that a better day
  Hath dawned on human kind,
Which teaches true philosophy—
  The science of the mind.

AN APOSTROPHE TO TIME.

Thou awful power whose mystic touch
   Marks with decay the works of man,—
What finite power has done so much,—
   What finite mind thy power can scan?
With scythe in hand, and forehead bare,
   When first the sun lit up this sphere,
On wing elastic as the air
   Thou didst commence thy swift career.
Great universal Leveler,
   Thy power is not confined to space;
Thou tireless, ceaseless traveler,
   Through all the earth, thy steps we trace.

Proud cities, arches, temples, domes—
   Which bid defiance to thy sway,
Like frost-work, where the sunbeam comes—
   Are crumbling, wasting, day by day;
And man, ere half he's run his race,
   His head with age thou silverest o'er;

Dost spread strange paleness o'er his face,
   And from his limbs extract their power.
The eye, where genius flashes bright—
   The cunning hand, the inventive mind—
They, too, must feel thy withering blight—
   To dark oblivion be consigned.

The muse of history weeps thy power—
   Not even she their names can save;
She holds them up their fleeting hour,
   And then thou hid'st them in that grave—
Thy treasure-house, where thou hast lain
   Names dear to fame in days of yore;
Deep, dark concealed, they must remain
   'Till thy devasting reign is o'er.
On tireless wing, still thou wilt rove,
   And pluck from his high sphere the sun;
Blot out each star that shines above,
   And then Eternity will come!

Duration measureless!—how vast!
   Vain, vain, O Time, thine efforts all;
Eternity! Eternity!!
   Shall wrap thee in its darkened pall.

A WISH.

That I might walk on earth
   As walked God's holy Son;
That every day might close
   With all its duties done.

That every winged hour,
   Laden, might bear to heaven
Thank-offerings, rich and pure,
   For hourly blessings given;

And this my motto ever be,
   Whate'er befalls me 'neath the sun,
Righteous art thou, thou God of love,
   Oh! not my will, but thine, be done.

I would have charity for all,
   Live holy, harmless, undefiled,
Tho' often tempted, sorely tried,
   Revile not, though I'm oft reviled.

I'd shun the gay and brilliant throng,
   Yet no lone hermitess would be;

But often spend delightful hours
   With souls of sweet affinity.

I would not turn away from one,
   Tho' most degraded of our kind,
If I could give one ray of light,
   Or healing for the darkened mind.

Nor, " be ye fed, and be ye clothed,"
   Would say to those who seek my door;
But, help to bear the grievous load
   Of God's benighted poor.

I'd leave my bed at dead of night
   To ease one throbbing brow or heart;
Would brave the storm, the cold, or heat,
   To bear some kindly part.

I would forgive the deepest wrong,
   As God hath oft forgiven me,
Knowing that motive is the test,
   And that's not given us to see.

SUMMER FRIENDS.

Close up the doors, shut out the world,
  The cold, vain, dark, deceptive scene,
Where, sick to faintness, waiting long,
  Each day, from earth, my heart doth wean.

Oh for some island in the sea,
  Some sweet green isle, where none intrude
To break, with vain pretensive smile,
  The silence of my solitude.

Yet, one true heart, amidst the wreck
  Of what I fondly dreamed was true,
Remains; and oh! it must be there,
  On that green speck of ocean blue.

The seamew's notes would charm my ear,
  And halcyons lull my soul to rest;
E'en 'midst the raging of the sea,
  I'd feel that I was richly blest.

Oh! for that haven of repose,
  Where no deceptive foot hath trod;
Oh! for that fold where lamblike souls
  Repose forever with their God.

"FAIN WOULD I FLY AWAY, AND BE AT REST."

O for that haven of repose
   Where lion-foot hath never trod,
Which vulture's eye hath never seen,
   And where the pure in heart see God.

Fain would I leave this dusty road,
   Which I so long have halting trod,
Would lay aside my pilgrim-staff,
   And dwell in heaven with God.

O hush my heart, and rather seek
   To be resigned; 'tis all of God,—
Yield meekly to his righteous will,
   And humbly kiss the rod.

All living things which move and breathe,
   From the poor reptile, 'neath the sod,
To the adoring hosts above,
   All have one source—that source is God.

Wisely he marks out every path;
   The thorn, the rose, the staff, the rod,
Alike are given us in love;
   Then, O my soul! trust thou in God.

THE HEART.

The heart! the heart! the human heart,
Its hidden mysteries who can tell?
Who can unclasp its mystic seal—
Its hopes, its fears, its love reveal?
Its bitter anguish who can see?
None but the eye of Deity.

That Power which formed its secret springs,
And woke to joy its tuneful strings,
Molded with plastic hand its form,
And sends life's current gushing warm
Throughout its chambers, dark and deep,
Will evermore its issues keep:
He feels each shock of joy or grief,
And knows the balm which brings relief.

The heart! the heart! the stony heart,
Made hard by sin, neglect, and scorn;
Devoid of pity, joy, and love,—
Bleak, dreary desert, dark, forlorn,
Unfeeling as the flinty stone;
Cold, isolated, dark, and lone.

The heart! the heart! the contrite heart,
Which lowly kneels to be forgiven,
Awakes a louder, sweeter note
Amid the angel choir in heaven;
A censer-flame, which warmly burns
When the poor prodigal returns.

The heart! the heart! the broken heart!
A moonbeam resting on the dead
Is like its smile, so fixed and cold
We know that every joy has fled,
A shattered lyre whose notes are flown;
Leave not the bleeding heart alone:
Thy balm of sympathy impart,
And O bind up the broken heart.

The heart! the heart! the trusting heart,
Confiding as the harmless child,
Ere the deceptive scenes of earth
Its trusting spirit hath beguiled;
It gives its fears unto the dust,
And heaven rewards the filial trust.

The heart! the heart! the hoping heart,
How dark soe'er its cloud of gloom,
A rainbow spans its threatening form,
And heavenly voices hither come,
Whispering, "Cheer up, I'm near to aid;
Behold, 'tis I, be not afraid."

The heart! the heart! the loving heart,
On sympathy and love it lives—
In every sorrow takes a part—
Its sympathy and love it gives;
Throws out its tendrils, like the vine,
Round loving spirits close doth twine;
Yet for a holier love it yearns,
Until the dust to dust returns.

The heart! the heart! the cheerful heart!
A harp of many thousand strings,
Whose music breaks the dismal spell
Pale melancholy round us flings;
Perpetual sunshine smiles around
Where'er the cheerful heart is found;
The evening fireside! O how sweet
The converse when such hearts do meet.

The heart! the heart! the pure in heart!
Ah! they alone behold their God;
Their pilgrim feet pursue the path
Which the Immaculate hath trod.
The dove of peace doth make its nest
Within the pure and stainless breast,
And joys divine to them are given,
While they sojourn from earth to heaven.

FOOTPRINTS.

On the mountains, in the vallies,
In the desert, every sod
Has been pressed by blessed footsteps,
Which have labored there for God.
Some with carnal weapons fight,
Yet no less secure the right.
Devious paths and various motives
Have been followed here and there;
Toiling ever, all his creatures
Still are busy everywhere.
Thus it is for God we labor,
Tho' most times we're unaware.

Thou who guid'st the tiny swallow
Thro' the crystal depths of air,
Hold'st the hearts of all thy creatures—
Beings of thy tenderest care.
Thou mak'st a path for every footprint—
Mak'st a foot to travel there:
Thou art love, and truth, and wisdom,
Thou art knowledge, power, and might;

Thou who nevermore permitteth
Aught but what thou see'st is right,
(While each one doeth as he willeth)
Holdest each by thine own might.

A glorious temple is being builded;
All we, thine agents, in it share,
Just the work in that grand temple
Which thy wisdom doth prepare;
And when the top stone's laid upon it,
All thy creatures will be there,
Shouting, "Grace, grace unto it,"
Thrilling heaven's holy air.

"THE MORNING STARS SANG TOGETHER."

Bright morning stars, how sweet ye chimed
    When first the world begun!
But there is much ye did not sing,
    Which never has been sung.

Which waiteth for the eternal morn,
    When all the human race
Begin the jubilatic song,
    Thrilling infinite space.

There is one song ye could not sing,—
    The angels sang it, when
They sang o'er Bethlehem, one glad night,
    Peace and good will to men.

Yet there's a song ye've ever sang,
    Ye blessed stars above,
And ye are chanting it to-night—
    That anthem, "God is love."

Be this the burden of your theme,
    O hymn it o'er and o'er,

While I, with hands and heart upraised,
  Stand silent and adore.

Soon sin and death will be destroyed,
  And righteousness abound,
When, from center to circumference,
  This glad song will resound.

MEMORY.

Ah! there are things we would forget,
   And shroud beneath oblivion's veil,
While sweetest joys we cherish yet,—
   As soon our hopes of heaven might fail.

As we forget them—nevermore!
   They are linked with life's mysterious tie;
They'll go with us to yonder shore,
   And swell our sum of bliss on high.

Here are they nestling like the dove
   Of peace, in hearts which oft have bled,
Restoring scenes of joy and love,
   And bringing back the sainted dead.

Hail memory, hold thine high domain!
   With sweet-voiced hope the soul inspire!
Illumine life, cheer and sustain,
   And warm it with thine hallowed fire!

THE GHOST OF UNREST.

Onward, O onward! Time in thy flight,
And turn thou not back,—not e'en "for to-night."
May there be light in the path which leads down
    the hill,
Down the dark valley—that valley so still.

O draw the dim curtain a little aside,—
Let me look thro' its folds where the sweet waters
    glide,—
Pray just let me see the delectable hill,
Where "remaineth a rest," so peaceful and still,—

Where float the soft notes on the heavenly breeze,
Whence come odors divine from the life-healing
    trees;
O I'm weary, I'm weary of this haunting unrest,
And fain would I go to the isles of the blest.

Here, if love ever folds its light, joyous wings
Round some warm kindred heart, and hopefully
    sings,
There reposing in peace, like the dove on its nest,
Then obtrusive it comes—the ghost of unrest.

Like the bee's restless wing midst the honeyed
  flowers,
Ever restless the soul with its angelic powers;
Yet when it leans on our Father's compassionate
  breast,
It ventures not there—the grim ghost of unrest.

LINES.

[Written on a centenarian woman, who was, for a long time, impressed with the idea that God had forgotten to take her out of the world, at which thought she grieved incessantly, until the worn out heart-strings broke, and the glad spirit, like an uncaged bird, flitted to its final rest.]

Poor homesick soul, bowed down with grief,
    Far on thy pilgrim journey come,
An infant of a hundred years,
    Art wildly crying to go home.

Far in thy second childhood now,
    Weary and tired, thy way-worn feet,
Thou hast borne the burden of life's day,
    Its morning chills and noontide heat.

Lone one!—companion, children gone,
    Thou hast outlived both kith and kin;
One by one, long years ago,
    The Father's house have entered in.

I am pained for thee, O aged one!
    I feel thy lonely agony;

Who knows but two-score years may pass,
　　And I be lone like thee?

Faintly thy feeble mind reverts
　　To tender scenes which love recalls;
For dim the lamp of memory burns,
　　In its deserted halls.

Thy household gods have turned to clay,
　　All crumbled by relentless time;
All gone the joys of early years,
　　And those of life's gay prime.

Bent is thy once tall, graceful form,
　　Thy locks are white as fallen snow,
And thou art blind, and deaf, and lame,—
　　We marvel not that thou would'st go.

O it is well we can depart,
　　And leave the suffering clay behind,
To join the loved of other years,—
　　Our God, our heaven, and home to find.

Thy withered hand, instinctive, holds
　　Thy bridal, time-worn ring;
May it go with thee to the dust,—
　　It is a sacred thing.

The satin slippers thou hast kept,
   So white, so trim, and neat,
Which trip'd the gay, fantastic toe,
   Upon thy bridal feet.

Moth-eaten are thy dainty robes,
   Which thou did'st wear in woman pride,
When, arm in arm, thou used to walk
   With him who long since died.

Dark dust is on the volumes now
   Which once were thy delight,
When thine eye was bright as the gazelle's,
   And all undimmed thy sight.

The music of thy loved guitar
   No more is heard within thine walls;
All mute are thy sweet singing birds,
   And dim the pictures on the walls.

Thine house-top, all o'ergrown with moss,
   Its walls are tottering to decay,
And desolation tracks the paths
   Where thou and thine did love to stray.

And thou art pining to go home;
   Earth's fruits are bitter to thy taste;
Yet fearing God's forgotten thee,
   Forgot to call thee to the feast.

Dear saint, the mother may forget
   Her child, or thrust it from her arms:
Yet never will thy God forget,—
   Thou art graven on his heart and palms.

Tenderer by far than human love,
   The love which warms the Father's breast,
And all his attributes are pledged
   To bring thee to his heaven of rest.

PRE-EXISTENCE.

["Methinks that we have known some former state more glorious than the present; and the heart is haunted by dim memories—shadows left by past felicity."]

Why do such memories haunt us?—
  Did our unclothed spirit dwell
'Neath the shadow of the tree of life,
  By the heavenly asphodel?

Are we only exiles here,
  Pilgrims in a world of strife,
Till mercy's hand unbars the gate,
  And gives us back our native life?

Have we lived in some other world
  Ere we were sent to this?
Or else, why does our spirit pine
  For joy it seems to miss?

Where is the heavenly, priceless pearl—
  The gem of perfect ray,—
The rose exhaling the sweet breath
  Of immortality?

The bird with pensive eyes
  Which cometh at our call,
Which bears not on its gladsome wing
  A trace of Eden's fall?

Our heart seems seeking something lost,—
  There's ever on the lip a prayer,
And stretching forth of empty hands,
  Which only grasp the air.

It seeks, until the eyes grow dim,
  To catch the slightest glance
Of what doth to vague memory seem
  A lost inheritance.

From the sanctuary of the soul
  Ascends, like altar-fires,
"Thoughts that breathe, and words that burn,"
  With vehement desires.

Like a blind worm feeling for wings
  Which its true instinct craves,
Or restless sunbeams in the dark
  Of subterranean caves.

Within our spirit's deep recess,
  Remains unsung our sweetest song;
Perhaps reserved for other worlds,
  It may not unto this belong.

AN AUTUMNAL WREATH.

Like some sweet rill beneath the ground,
   Which is not fed by dew or rain,
It sometimes breathes low murmurings,
   Yet we have never caught its strain.

Could we but breathe from out our soul
   A song aglow with holy fires,
Never to cease the heart to thrill
   Till time itself expires;

But on some hallowed mission sent,
   Might waft wherever man hath trod,
An offering laid at Jesus' feet,
   And consecrated unto God.

Till then, we never can attain
   The height of our desires;
And in our prisoned souls must burn
   Its useless, pent-up fires.

There is a hungering of the soul
   No earthly manna can allay;
A longing for untasted bliss,
   Not subject to decay.

Dear God, if thou hast sent us here
   To wait, to labor, and to learn,
May faith suffice, instead of sight,
   Till to thy bosom we return.

From round to round may we ascend
  Until so near the skies,
Pure, white-robed souls, at eventide,
  Look full into our eyes.

THE PARTING HOUR.

Sister beloved, O must we part?—
   To me the thought is hard to bear,
It brings a pang into the heart,
   Into the eye a tear.

A tear which I would fain suppress,
   Or wholly hide from thee;
I would no thought might thee distress,
   However painful 'tis to me.

I know that many tender ties
   Attract thee to thy native home,
That loving hearts and wishful eyes,
   Impatient, wait for thee to come.

Would it had been our lot to live
   United, as in time that's fled,
Loving, as when in babyhood,
   We nestled in our trundle-bed.

When a mother's tender love
   Our hands did in her bosom warm,

And a loving, sainted sire
    Did shield his charge from harm.

As when, on unshod feet, we strayed
    Upon the dewy grass at morn,
Or in the mellow sunlight, played
    Among the ripened corn.

When we would chase the birds and bees
    Far down the stream we loved so well,
And in our childhood's laughing glee
    Our funny stories tell.

Ah me! how death has thin'd our ranks!
    The clover grows o'er loving lips,
And eyes, which fondly beamed on us,
    Are veiled in dark eclipse.

Like statues in a marble niche,
    They stand in mem'ry's undimmed halls,
And look with loving eyes on us,
    Upon our pictured walls.

Sister, the years press hard on us;
    Life's uplands now seem hard to climb;
While in the flowerless vale I wait
    For life's last sunset chime.

But thou must go — say not farewell;
   The parting hour will soon be o'er, —
The train is near, I hear the bell,
   Which seems to say, we meet no more.

Yet we shall meet where no sad bell
   Shall ever warn us more to part:
Now one fond kiss, beloved, farewell,
   Sister, farewell, we now must part.

ALONE.

[The following lines were written in answer to a friend who inquired if I was ever lonesome when alone.]

O friend! I never am alone,
    Nor do I hope to ever be;
And when you deem me all alone,
    The loved in life are still with me.

Alone!—how can one feel alone
    When God's sweet peace pervades the breast?
The vacant head and heart are lone,
    As lone as a forsaken nest

When the sweet bird has flown away,
    In other climes to build and sing,
And silence in its native tree
    Lists for the tender notes of spring.

O I have felt more lonely far
    Within the gay, thronged, festive hall,
Than now, while gazing at yon star,
    And listening to the waterfall

Which lifts its pensive voice on high,
    And mingles with the night birds' songs;
While echo, from the distant hills,
    The solemn sound prolongs.

And I have felt a deeper thrill,
    A holier impulse o'er me steal,
When all the world lay locked in sleep,
    And night its glories did reveal.

I've ever loved to gaze at night,
    Into the silent depths of even,—
To mark the watch-fires all ablaze
    Along the high out-posts of heaven.

I joy at the calm noon of night,
    With sweet peace pillowed on the heart,
When myriad voices swell with praise,
    To bear a silent part.

There's a love within my inmost soul
    Which holds communion deep and high,
With all forms of life, from the crawling worm
    To the bright seraph of the sky.

I love to roam in forests dim,
    And list to nature's grand refrain,
Now hushed in death-like silence deep,
    When, lo! the chorus swells again,

Making the very silence feel
  The intenseness of an awful power,
Which to the inmost soul explains
  The language of the leaf and flower.

The leaves, I've pressed them to my lips,
  In love with nature more than art,
Whispering, "the hand which fashioned these,
  Moulded my beating heart.

O green, green leaves and fragrant flowers!
  O swelling buds with bursting hearts!
God's smiles are ye,—ye seem to form
  Of earthly love and heaven a part.

I ever feel in these dim aisles,
  To kneel on meekly bended knees,
While soft winds, like cathedral choirs,
  Warble amidst the trees.

Where could I fly to be alone?—
  For should the wings of morning bear
Me far beyond the setting sun,
  Lo! the dear God is there.

Should I descend Tartarean depths,
  Where never human foot hath trod,
E'en in that solemn, dark abode,
  I still should be with God.

AN AUTUMNAL WREATH.

Beloved, I would not be alone,—
   I love the converse of a friend,—
Most dear the hours I pass with thee,
   Thy soul and mine together blend.

A cloistered nun I would not be,
   A hermit life I do not crave;
To me true friendship is a boon,
   The richest gift kind heaven e'er gave.

A gift in love and mercy sent
   To keep alive the human heart;
Hast thou one friend?—Cherish the gift,
   Nor with thy life's best treasure part.

TO MY MOTHER, ON MY MARRIAGE.

Mother, farewell! I go from thee,
    Like the dove from the sheltering ark;
Henceforth another hand than thine
    Will guide my fragile bark.

Another voice will counsel me,
    Inspiring courage, hope sublime,
Another heart will sympathize
    In fortune's adverse time.

'Tis hard, indeed, to say farewell,
    Oh, best of mothers mine!—
No heart can ever beat for me
    More tenderly than thine.

Thy faithful heart, thy gentleness,
    Thy tender care and love,
Hath woke a chord within my soul
    To thrill in worlds above.

Their memory will be to me,
    Sweet as spring violet's breath;

Held sacred in my inmost heart
    Through life—nor lost in death.

I look upon thy pensive brow,
    Upon thy silvery hair,
And feel that in thine aged heart,
    A sadness gathers there.

I go, perchance, to joy—to weep,—
    For such is human lot;
But be my future what it may,
    I ne'er shall be forgot.

If one loved heart should cease to beat,
    That heart on which my hope doth rest,
Then will thy mateless bird return
    Back to its native nest.

TO AN OLD SCHOOLMATE.

My early friend, I mourn thy fall;
   Better for thee that thou had died,
With all thy laurels on thy brow,
   In thy young manhood's pride.

O cursed forever be the bowl
   Which lures with sparkles at the brim,
Yet, in its poisoned depths doth hold
   The germ of every sin.

And O I feel, most sorely feel,
   That thou, a child of destiny,
Did see, and hate, yet could not shun
   The path which led to infamy.

Thou seemest like a fallen star,
   A darkened, smouldering spark,
More useless than the mimic light
   Of glow-worm in the dark.

Science has lost a votary,
   The sick thy skill to tend.

Religion grieves at thy sad fall,
    Thy country mourns a friend.

Once I loved thee with a childish love,
    Thy manners were so mild;
Thou wast the idol of our school,
    At home a favorite child.

As comely as an Adonis,
    Thou wast in form and face,
With the light of genius in thine eye,
    Which, in vain, I strive to trace.

I've buried deep within my soul
    The hopes which thy young life inspired;
Drank deep of the oblivious stream,
    Since those high hopes expired.

And now farewell; O nevermore
    Would I see thee again,
So painful and so mournfully
    Renewing memory's chain.

And as, in the long years, I've lived
    Afar away from thee,
So would I still, and fain forget
    Thy sad apostasy.

And yet, fond memory will not sleep,
   But in the mirror of the past
Beholds thee, with exalted aims,
   Too high and bright, to last.

And still my prayer will be for thee,—
   Who knows but heaven may yet restore
Thee to thy former self again,
   And to thy friends once more.

'Tis vain, indeed, to think to stand,
   Without a trust in heaven and prayer;
It is to carve our names on sand,
   Or write them on the desert air.

TO ONE IN HEAVEN.

Back through the vista of long years
   I look and see a well-known face,
Whose name is graven on my heart
   In lines which time can ne'er efface.

Sweet cherished vision, stay! O stay!
   Thou rapture-breathing spell!
Fond memory lingering o'er the past
   Hath kept her record well.

Through all my varied walks of life,
   Through fortune, good or ill,
'Midst joyful scenes or suffering days,
   Thine image haunts me still.

Thine was a heart of purest mold;
   A high, aspiring soul was thine;
Not merely to be great, but good;
   Rather to glow than shine.

Mild was thine eye as parting day,
   Or my loved star at even;

And thy sweet smile of tenderness
  Seemed less of earth than heaven.

And shall I see that face in heaven?
  And will it look to me the same?
Wilt thou not meet me at the gate,
  And call me by my angel-name?

Hopes, long since gathered up to die,
  And flowers which drooped in early prime,
May yet re-bloom in some bright world,
  And swell its harvest-time.

I know not where that region lies,
  Where thy glad feet now roam:
Yet be that place where'er it may,
  'Twill be my heaven, my home.

COME UP HIGHER.

Come up higher!—they beckon me,
    With snowy hands — those gone before; —
For those whom they loved in this world of ours,
    They will love for evermore.

They stand by the side of the river of life,
    Where the waters so softly flow,
Yet wishfully look down the valley of death,
    For those whom they left long ago.

In heaven they look on their crucified Lord,
    Where is hallowed every desire,
And they look down below, where the dark shadows
        rest,
    And continually beckon me higher.

Like those who roam o'er the burning sands,
    And long for the cooling stream,
Or as exiles, from their country torn,
    See home in every dream.

So I dream, and long for that world of rest
    Whence those sweet voices come;
Yet wait, my soul, the time of the Lord,
    Then strike home, O spirit, strike home!

LOVE WITHOUT ALLOY.

There is a chamber in my heart
  Which seldom holds a guest;
A bounteous table waiteth there,
  Yet few come to the feast.

The guest for which my spirit pines
  Is love,—pure, unalloyed,
Refined from all earth's dust and dross,—
  Naught else can fill the void.

Where soul with soul in love doth meet,
  Heart interchange with heart;
Where every feeling, taste, and wish,
  Doth find its counterpart.

Friendships broadcast are sown,—
  Such as the world calls so,—
Which, like the waves of ocean-tide,
  Do ever ebb and flow.

Friendships most tender, sweet, are mine,
  Love, which I know is real,

But O they fall so far below
  My glorious, high ideal.

Is it the yearning of a soul
  Allied to a holier sphere,
That thus it pines and grieves apart,
  Yet finds no echo here?

I have asked the night, as I have walked
  'Neath the burning stars on high,
And the strange voices of the spheres,
  But none gave a reply.

"Thou deep-voiced sea, hast thou," I cried,
  "In thy deep caverns kept
A heart which this priceless pearl hath found,
  And an eye which ne'er hath wept?"

And the sea, as it mirrored the genial sun,
  Gave out no answering tone,
But its waves, as they washed the pebbly shore,
  Like my own heart seemed to moan.

O sea, dost thou grieve when thy caves are full
  Of the wealth of earth's silver and gold?
When the genius and beauty of earth are thine,
  Which thou dost in thy bosom hold?

Ah! thy gulphing billows forever will yearn,
  For there is a restless void,
Like the aching void within my heart,
  Which pines for a love unalloyed.

Then I turned to the depth of my inmost soul,
  Thus vainly yearning here,
And it answered, "perfection is not of earth,—
  'Tis the growth of a holier sphere."

KINDRED SOULS.

There's a mysterious chord, which thrills
    When kindred spirits meet,—
Feelings unspoken, undefined,—
    So strange, and yet so sweet,

Which take possession of the soul,
    Before we are aware,
And seem far less of earth than heaven,—
    For heaven seems everywhere.

Who have not felt emotions strange,
    An undefined, mysterious thrill,
Which to themselves was unexplained,—
    So independent of the will?

When they have taken by the hand
    One whom they never met before,
Think ye such souls were not allied
    On some celestial shore?

Are they not those within whose breasts
    Each feeling finds an answering tone,—

Whose tender, throbbing hearts do feel
  The deep pulsations of our own?—

Who only live when we do live,
  Who seem to die whene'er we die;
Or if they linger when we're gone,
  Their lives are hid on high.

Should they depart for other worlds,
  Leave us in grief behind,
The law which binds our spirits here,
  In other worlds will bind.

THE FATHERLAND.

Are there not those we've here not met,
Whose memory lingers with us yet?
With whom we've wandered, hand in hand,
Beside the streams of fatherland?

Perhaps in some bright world of bliss,
Or ere we wandered into this,
We parted, as we left that sphere,
And sometimes meet while pilgrims here.

Like angel's visits, far between,
Seldom they come,—more seldom seen;
And yet vague recollections seem
Lingering, like some forgotten dream

Of something spoken or once heard,
Which deeply hath the spirit stirred,
Like psalms, heard by the quickened ear
Of dying saints, while leaving here.

When first awakened—when we've slept
A little while—we've often wept

At the quick flitting of a face,
Of which dim memory held some trace.

We breathe the fragrance of a flower,
Then dimly see some mystic bower,—
In vain we strive to think where seen
That sacred bower, so cool and green.

Music, sometimes, at eve's calm hour,
Comes with its sweet, enchanting power,
Borne on the twilight's dewy wing,—
This to the soul vague memories bring,—

Of quivering harps, and sweet-toned lyre,
Which once did set the soul on fire,
And makes us long to reach the strand
Of our dear native fatherland.

FRIENDSHIP.

I deem the holiest thing of earth
    That which has ne'er been soiled by sin;
That plant of healing sent from heaven
    To win us back again.

So vainly sought, so rarely given!—
    Friendship such as the angels name,
Those pure immortals of the skies,
    Who bask in its celestial flame.

'Tis there, in all its pristine glow,
    It poises up the seraph's wing;
Heaven's sweetest joys its highest bliss
    From their pure friendship spring.

Painful distrust can find no place
    Where mutual souls, as through a glass,
Behold its budding, opening bloom,
    While heaven's sweet seasons pass.

If aught on earth can hold me here,
    When vanished years have spent my prime,

It must be thine, O friendship dear!
   Heaven's sweet gift almost divine.

There is a fountain in my heart
   Which ever swelleth at thy name;
Its waters mingle when they meet,—
   From heaven's fount they came.

O there are souls who find a home
   Within my heart, its grief they calm;
When Marah's waters brim my cup,
   They pour the soothing balm.

Their very thoughts are with me still,
   Writ on my heart as in a book;
I hoard, with more than miser's care,
   Each cherished word and look.

I would not cull the scentless flower,
   With gaudy tints, imperial red;
Be mine the modest fragrant bloom,
   Whose sweetness lingers when 'tis dead.

When true friends die their memory lives,
   Survives within our heart of hearts,
Which, like the full-orbed setting sun,
   Lingers to bless e'er it departs.

LOST JEWELS.

[Time and death have been very busy; they have robbed me of some of the rarest jewels; but their precious memories are forever with me.—*Epistolary Correspondence.*]

How often, like the stricken fawn,
   I've sought the cooling shade,
To soothe the anguish of my heart,
   Which recent grief had made.

For ere life's early morn was past,
   The bird in my heart refused to sing,
And ere I gained youth's sunny height,
   She'd folded up her wing.

Whatever I had loved the best
   Was surely always first to go;
With me it has been ever thus,—
   'Tis for the best I know.

I had a lamb, an orphan lamb,
   Its wool as white as driven snow,
Its dove-like eyes, so calm and meek,
   And O it loved me so.

But it was gone ere half a year,
    That life so loved, so brief,—
Poignant the sorrow of that hour,
    For that was my first grief.

I had a tree of matchless form,
    Which fragrance shed from every leaf,
Whose life, like clouds of summer morn,
    Was beautiful and brief.

A rosebush graced my loved pateree,
    O'er which I oft with pleasure hung,
More beautiful and fragrant far
    Than ever Flora sung.

Too beautiful, alas! to stay;
    I scanned it with an anxious eye,
A worm was eating at its root,
    And soon that rose did die.

I had a friend whose little heart
    Responsive with my own did beat,
To school, to church, together went
    With cheerful hearts and willing feet.

As she walked out to gather flowers,
    One lovely morn in May,

AN AUTUMNAL WREATH.

Death gently waived his mystic wand,
   And turned my friend to clay.

I think my heart had harder grown;
   I could not grieve as when my pet,
My snow-white, meek-eyed orphan lamb
   Did close those eyes of jet.

And there was one whose heart of hearts
   Was fondly pledged in deathless trust,
Not many moons had waxed and waned
   Before that friend was dust.

The reaper, Death, with palid face,
   Came o'er our way with noiseless tread;
I sought that friend, that friend was not,
   A broken heart was mine instead.

'Twas when the hunter's moon hung high,
   And silvery rays were all afloat,
Two shining spirits passed it by,
   And sailed beyond the blue remote.

And when I knew that friend was dead,
   Nor longer seen my walks among,
"Eloi, lama, sabacthani,"
   Hung trembling on my tongue.

I had a bird, which sweetly sung
   Above our vine-wreathed door,
Too sweet, alas! to linger long,
   Too soon 'twas heard no more.

I had a gem—a spirit gem,—
   A bud of being, beauteous, rare;
I laid it on my heart, and when
   I looked again, it was not there.

Swiftly did the death-angel come,—
   A look of agony I cast,
A silent look of tender love,—
   It was the last,—the last.

Now often when the day is done,
   And twilight lingers in the west,
I count these jewels, one by one,
   Loving each one the best.

Yet there are jewels richer far
   Than time on earth can e'er reveal,
Hid far behind the morning star,
   'Till friendly death our eyes unseal.

MY ANGEL WATCHER.

A saintly form forever
  About our path doth keep,
That never leaves us—never!
  Whether we sleep or wake.

She walketh just behind us,
  With hand on either side,
And wings of purplish azure
  Protectingly spread wide.

She sitteth by our pillow,
  When sleep our eye doth close,
And patiently the livelong night
  She guardeth our repose.

At morn, some mystic presence
  Awakes us from our sleep,
And when no form we can discern,
  We almost feel to weep.

And thus she's always with us,
  In every time and place;

She is always just behind us,
   So we ne'er can see her face.

Bless God for this good angel,
   Who doth our footsteps guide;
And, until we cross the river,
   May she with us abide.

Oft she holds our feet from pitfalls,
   Which thick beset our way;
And saves from many hidden snares,
   Which in our path doth lay.

She cheers us when desponding,
   And, when weary, sick, and faint,
She leads to healing waters,—
   Our angel watcher, saint.

MOTHER LOVE.

Mother, fold me again to thy heart,
    Let me feel thy warm breath on my cheek;
The world groweth cold, and is drear,
    Now thy love, as in childhood, I seek.

That love which cradled me early,
    Which asked for naught in return,
But the babe-love borne in my bosom,
    Which in my ripe heart now doth burn.

O thy love, dearest mother, how holy!—
    'Tis a spark from the bosom of God,
More tender and warm now in heaven,
    While thy heart lieth under the sod.

My faith grasps the pillars of heaven;
    On what else can the sad heart recline?
Say, are there not many there gathered
    Who feel every heart-throb of mine?

OUR MOTHER.

"Oh, how we miss her!"*

Loved sister! — yes, we miss a form,
　A saintly form which we adored;
We do not miss her in our hearts,
　But in our home and at our board.

That saintly form is imaged on
　The retina of affection's eye,
And when that form grew cold in death,
　Part of our being seemed to die.

We miss a sympathizing breast,
　A mild and placid, pitying eye,
Which e'er to sorrow and distress
　Gave tear for tear and sigh for sigh.

* This was an expression of my sister's, in a letter which she addressed to me soon after our mother's death. It was the language of the soul speaking through its tears, in all the eloquence of grief. I can never recall them without a feeling of the deepest emotion; they touched the very tenderest chord of my whole being.

AN AUTUMNAL WREATH.

We miss a voice, whose accents fell
   On our glad ear, as falls the shower
Upon the parched and arid ground,
   Bringing to life the drooping flower.

We miss a hand, which grasped our own,
   Outside the door of that lov'd cot,
Whene'er we came,—and that sweet smile,
   Ah! *that* can never be forgot.

We miss a step, whose near approach
   Sent gladness bounding through our heart;
And homesick feelings o'er us came
   Whene'er we heard that step depart.

How, at the hour of morning prayer,
   That sacred hour when we all meet,
We miss that loved, that rev'rent form,—
   Like Mary's at the Master's feet.

How sad to us that vacant chair,
   Which on that lonely hearth remains,
Where grieves a widowed pilgrim gray,
   As grieves the dove whose mate is slain.

At nightfall,—how we miss her then,
   How lonesome seems the evening hearth:

Where can we go and miss her not?
  Nowhere upon the earth.

Sister, that voice which charmed our ear
  With its low cradle lullaby,
It is not lost,—in some bright world
  It swells with angel-melody.

The chord within that mother-heart,
  Which vibrates with affection deep,
With tender pity o'er us swells,
  While we in sadness weep.

Again to meet that tender friend,
  A joyful hope to us is given;
A few more sorrowing days,—and then
  We all shall meet in heaven.

MAY.

Month of my heart! and art thou here,—
    Here with thy warm and dewy wing,—
With brightening skies and weeping showers, —
    The very genii of the Spring;
And the sweet Redbreast has returned
    From his long tour o'er Southern plains,
And here recounts the homesick hours
    He had where slavery clanks her chains.

With all thy charms, thou lovely month,
    To me thou seem'st with tearful eye:
'Twas on thy lap, thou pensive queen,
    My mother laid her down to die!
Pale May-moon, thou art beauteous now,
    As in my days of childhood glee,—
I know no change has o'er thee come,
    'Tho' colder *seem* thy beams to me.

'Tis not the scenes on which we gaze
    That are so dim or are so bright,—
It is the medium,—the haze,
    Through which we view them,—dark or light,

When childhood's dew was on this brow,
    And the warm pulse of life beat high,
O how I sighed for thee, sweet May!
    When wintry winds went howling by.

And when I saw thy heralds come,—
    The gauzy cloud, the sky more blue;
And on the brown, frost-bitten sod,
    Saw the green grass come peeping through,
I thought it was earth's natal time,
    And she was keeping holy-day,
And she had called her minstrels out
    To swell the festive melody.

Then with my pet I wandered forth;
    (I had a pet, as I have now,—
A snow-white lamb—an orphan lamb;
    The pet I now have marks my brow.)
O blissful days of innocence!
    No sins to mourn or be forgiven;
If bliss so sweet, I know again
    It sure must be in heaven.

*THOUGH SORROW ENDURE FOR A NIGHT,
YET JOY COMETH IN THE MORNING.*

After the drought—the blessed rain,
Reviving the drooping flowers and grain,
The sun returns with cheering light
After the gloom of a starless night.

After the shower—the heavenly bow;
After the cold—the feathery snow;
After winter—buds and leaves,
And twittering swallows under the eaves.

After summer—the teeming horn,
Full of flowers and fruit and corn;
Then the frost-robed starry night,
When the harvest-moon hangs clear and bright.

After the harvest—rest from toil,
When the golden sheaves from the genial soil
Gladden all hearts, and offerings rise
Like the smoke of a grateful sacrifice.

After the shroud—the wedding vest;
After the corse, the bride is dress'd;
For joy doth ever follow pain,
As after the drought the blessed rain.

After the day—the silent night,
When the downy couch doth to rest invite;
When o'er the frame soft slumbers creep,
For "He giveth his beloved sleep."

After the battle—the warriors rest
Side by side with the pulseless breast
That burns no more with a deadly hate;
Tho' peace has come, it has come too late.

After bondage—liberty comes;
After oppression—peaceful homes,
When 'neath the shade of the fruitful vine
Unfettered forms in peace recline.

After the sigh—the radiant smile;
After sickness—health awhile,
When the rose doth bloom on the cheek again,
And hopes revive which in dust had lain.

After adieus and farewells spoken—
After the golden bowls are broken—

Beyond the river joyful greetings,
And holiest of all holy meetings.

After the sorrows of life are past,
And the grief-worn heart hath grieved its last.
When death at length the eye doth close,
Then comes the joy of heaven's repose.

THE OLD CARPET.

"Yes, take the dusty thing away."
To patient Mary I said one day.
As o'er its time-worn form I careless walked,
And of its faded roses mused and talked.

While near at hand a new bought carpet lay,
To take the old one's place, whenever borne away;
Waiting, impatient, soon to find its place,
The gaudy stranger stared me in the face,

As if the floral goddess had let fall
A shower of lilies, roses, leaves and all,
In such profusion, that one seemed to smell
Their very odors as they rose and fell.

Each swelling bud seemed waiting to disclose
Its folded petals, and become a rose;
And then the shaded leaves, with green so rare,
Seemed as if Nature's plastic hand was there.

"Yes, take the dusty thing away,
And in its place the new one smoothly lay;
Indeed, I'm tired of this poor faded thing,
So hasten, Mary, and the new one bring."

This my reproving angel heard;
And quick as thought my heart was stirred,
Suggesting what the thing had been,
And how admired, when first 'twas seen.

And thoughts came rushing thick and fast,
Of joyous scenes,—of pleasure's past,—
And heaven-like notes seemed lingering near,
Which oft had thrilled my raptured ear.

"O thou, the old, I love thee still,"
I said,—and said it with good will;
Now, as old friends pass in review,
The old seems better than the new.

Old friends which cleave unto my heart,
Who of my soul do form a part,
Have often made each heart more dear
By converse sweet while lingering here.

Upon thine ancient faded form,
Where shone the hearth-fire, bright and warm,
When none thy soiled flowers once upbraided,
Or even thought thy roses faded.

Feet, which have mingled with the dust,
Voices, which death long since have hushed,
Eyes, which my sorrows have beguiled,
Lips, which in love have on me smiled,

All, all come back,—they're here, they're here!
Thrice blest, old carpet,—thou art dear!
Nor thy successor e'er can share
The love for thee my heart doth bear,

Since thou dost call back other hours,
Which in my heart, like fragrant flowers,
Were all wrapt up and lain away;—
Yet thou hast ope'd them here to-day,

And scattered them all o'er the room;
O how thy colors do re-bloom!—
More lovely far than is the new!—
And, like old friends, till death art true.

OUR HOME.

Affection sanctifies this place,
   From which my feet do seldom roam;
Here cluster thick my sweetest joys,
   Beneath thy peaceful roof, "sweet home."

The dove of peace here hath her nest;
   Here, evermore, may she abide;
She drops not in, a stranger guest,
   But still is ever at our side.

Hallowed to me is each loved spot;
   Each flower or shrub I love to tend
Recalls some dear, remembered scene,
   Some dearly loved or long-lost friend.

O how I love thy sylvan shades!
   The winding stream which murmurs by!
Thine ancient elms and towering pines,
   Which seem to almost meet the sky!

I love them for "Our Father's sake,"—
   They speak his love,—all show his power,—

From the tall pine which nods his praise
   Down to the very tiniest flower.

Around the casements of our home
   I love to rear the clustering vine;
Amidst its foliage, cool and green,
   To help the honeysuckle twine.

'Tis meet that elegance and taste
   Should e'er surround our earthly home,
Where weary nature seeks repose,
   And eager feet so gladly come.

There is a sun that lights my home,
   Which is by far more dear than all,
And should that sun go down for age,
   O'er home 'twould throw a dismal pall.

I love, O yes, I dearly love,
   The quiet room where most I stay,
And muse, and write, and read, and sew,
   While pass the halcyon hours away.

Not she who rules on Albion's throne,
   With cringing millions at her feet,
Such sweet content can call her own,
   As I, within my home retreat.

Then hail, sweet home! forever dear!
　Thou peaceful cot! thou calm retreat!
Where love, and hope, and faith sincere,
　Take sanctuary sweet.

LINES.

[Written on returning from a journey.]

Like the bird to its eyrie,
    Like the dove to its nest,
I return to thy bosom,
    Thou dear place I love best.

Sweet home of my heart,
    Here I'll rest for awhile
'Midst thy green, cooling shades,
    And affection's sweet smile.

Long since did I leave thee
    To wander abroad,
'Mid scenes of rare beauty
    My glad feet have trod.

I have grasped the warm hand
    Of friendship most dear,
And have wept o'er the grave
    The sorrowing tear.

Now like the bird to its eyrie,
　Or the dove to its nest,
I come back to thy bosom
　For quiet and rest.

OUR GARDEN.

Our garden, blooming with sweet grace,
    Oft woes us to its loved retreat
With odors as from Indian groves,
    Where lovliest hues in contrast meet,

As if the rainbow had come down,
    The calm inviting scene to share;
Trailing its gorgeous drapery round,
    Had left its colors there.

The white rose, queen of all the flowers,
    As sweet as sweet can be,
And bright-eyed, golden buttercups
    Which came from o'er the sea.

The gaudy peonies, all ablaze,
    Laughing up to the very eyes;
While by their side the *fleur de lis*
    Has caught the hue of the summer-skies.

Joseph's coat of many colors,
    Mourning wreath for mourning bride,

While Narcissus, pale and love-lorn,
   Languish by their side.

Vials of odors, in pale green,
   The pink-buds, scenting all the air,
Like censers waved by holy hands,
   When hearts gush forth in prayer.

Like vesper-bells, in other climes,
   The hair-bells slowly swinging,
While nestling 'neath its tiny tongue
   The honey-bee is singing.

Pale violets, hid beneath the shade,
   Breathing their sweetness on the air,
Modest and meek as lovliest maid,
   Or Samuel knelt in prayer.

This willow graced Helena's Isle,
   Where slept the warrior chief,
An exile, on his broken shield,
   A blot on life's last leaf.

The south wind long doth linger here,
   The quiet scene adorning,
Rocking the drowsy night to sleep,
   And waking up the morning.

Birds so tamely flying low
  They almost sweep my hair,
Then, sweetly singing, off they go
  Into the ambient air.

Earth's holiest bird has built her nest
  Within a sheltering lime;
Here her unswaddled infants rest
  Lull'd by the south wind's chime.

Young, half-dressed birds oft hurry here
  On wings of earliest light,
Lisping their sonnets all day long,
  Go home to roost at night.

These beautious things, of my warm love,
  All share a generous part;
But the pale rose I evermore
  Will wear upon my heart.

My heart does talk, ere I'm aware,
  To flowers, and birds, and bees,
And fain would build its altar here
  Amidst these whispering trees.

Three tabernacles here I'd build;
  The first, to Him who paints the flowers;

The next to dearest friends;
   One, to the muse, who, midst these bowers,
Her genial influence lends.

I love to think that God is here
   Within this calm retreat;
To pluck the rarest, choicest flowers,
   And lay them at His feet.

Jesus the garden dearly loved,—
   'Twas there he meekly prayed,
And in a hallowed garden, too,
   His form in death was laid.

FLOWERS.

[It has been beautifully remarked by some one, that "flowers are God's smiles."]

God's finger touched it,—lo, it bloomed!
   This little dainty thing!
A gem upon the breast of morn!
   Just on the verge of Spring.

It has been said "flowers are God's smiles;"
   I'm glad if so,—so may it be.
How sweet, when I admire a flower,
   To feel He smiles on me.

The meek-eyed violet of the vale,
   The wild rose in deep solitudes,
Are His sweet smiles on us, on all,
   And speak his rich beatitudes.

When the wild ox roams the prairie,
   And snuffs the balmy air,
Mirrored in his great wild bright eyes,
   The smiles of God appear.

Often I've thought, when I have seen
    A mother feed her child,
When she would add some simple flower,
    Saying, "take this, love," with looks so mild.

Of Him, who when he's fed and clothed
    Us, children of his love,
Addeth the many-tinted flowers
    To raise our hearts above.

When he had grown the tasseled corn,
    And clustering fruit upon the vine,
Our garners filled with golden grain,
    And poured the generous wine.

A Father's love, still undefined,
    Which height nor depth can know,
As if unsatisfied with these,
    Gave them a simpler love to show.

Thus He ten thousand blessings still
    Into our laps doth pour,
Until our hands and hearts are full
    Of blessings, running o'er.

THE BLACK CRICKET.

Little cricket at thy matins,
    Darkey, harping with thy harp,
There's nothing soft about thy singing,
    But all is sharp, sharp.

So sharp, it cuts the hours in two,
    Making two of one;
Little dark-complexioned sinner,
    When wilt thou be done?

My ears are aching, and my nerves
    Are wide awake to-night;
Say, little harper, is thy song
    To last till morning light?

There, thou art still. I now can rest;
    Soft slumbers o'er me creep;
Thankful I am thy song has ceased,—
    O come refreshing sleep!

Ah, here it comes again,—so sharp!
    O scissors, razors, knives!

Not only cutting hours in two,
   But sleep, distracted, flies.

Well, I will lie and think of Him
   Who made thee with thy harp;
Perhaps 'tis best I wake and muse,—
   So harp thee, darkey, harp.

Then sing, thou merry little one,
   Chant thy sharp notes of glee!
The One who doth inspire thy song,
   Careth for thee and me.

TO A STUFFED DUCK.

The hand of love first brought thee here,
Where thou hast stood for many a year,
Looking as life-like, pert, and trim,
As ducks which on the water swim.

Thou art a pretty bird, indeed;
   That's all of thee I know, no more;
I've wished I could thy history read,
   While I have scanned thee o'er and o'er.

O say, art thou a bird of yore,
   Or wast thou hatched in modern times?—
Art thou a native of our shore,
   Or emigrant from other climes?

Perhaps some Indian, as he roamed
   To hunt the deer and wild roe-buck,
Espied thee on some forest lake,
   And shot thee dead, thou pretty duck.

And thy dear mate and ducklings, too,
   Perhaps were with thee on the wave,

And saw thee die, and sighed adieu,
  While flying off, dear life to save.

When the big Indian clutched thy neck,
  And bore thy bleeding form away,
And made thee just the wondrous thing
  Which thou art here to-day.

Did he not bear thee to his tent,
  Where his dear squaw thy form admired,
And so to please her taste refined
  Fixed thee just as she then desired?—

So took from thee thy tender heart,
  Ere death had scarcely stilled its beat,
Then stuffed with moss thy downy skin,
  And varnished o'er thy pretty feet?—

Took from thine head thy beauteous eyes,
  Which gazed so wistfully on him,
And gave thee eyes of glass instead?—
  Alas! their sight, how dim!

Well, changes come to birds, and all;
  And I, too, of the lordly race
Shall change, and in the distant years
  Some curious eye may trace

A semblance of a skull or hand,—
A lock of hair,—a tooth or nail,—
Wondering to whom they once belonged,—
But all their search may fail.

Except to hint, one lived and died,—
Just this, and nothing more.
Help us, high heaven, our vanity
And weakness to deplore.

A TALK WITH A BLUE VIOLET BY MOONLIGHT.

By a hawthorn hedge where the dewdrops shone,
Where 'twas cold and damp,—the snow just gone,
A flower peeped out 'midst its leaves of green—
'Twas the violet blue, spring's modest queen.

Meek-eyed dweller of the lowly vale,
Why droops thy form 'neath the moonbeams pale?
Why low on the ground thy soft blue eye,
Dwellers of the valley, O tell me why?

Nestling 'midst diamond and pearly dew,
Thyself a gem of cerulean hue,
Yet, lowly and quiet, modest and meek,
The praise of the passers thou scornest to seek.

And tho' fragrance and gold* and beauty are thine,
Down low in the valley thy head doth recline;

*Mr. R. Hunt, of the London Royal Institution, stated that a friend of his had succeeded in obtaining a minute, though weighable, portion of gold from a quantity of the petals of the blue violet.

And as I bend o'er thee, thou art whispering to me,
"Humility should dwell with frailty."

O beautiful lesson, abide in my heart!
Sweet floral apostle, instruction impart!
Beautiful violet—child of the sod!
Thou dost teach *me humility* and dependence on
    God.

"Tho' pavilioned midst verdure of emerald hue,
And thou call'st me a gem of cerulean blue,
Yet, ephemeral my life, each moment that flies
Is a star that has set never more to arise."

SUMMER EVE.

Sweet summer eve—I e'er must be
To thy loved charms a devotee;
When the mother-bird to her nestlings come,
And toil-worn feet are hurrying home.

When the floral censers their incense yield,
And perfume goes up from the clover-field,
And the dew descends like an answering word,
And tells each flower that its prayer is heard.

When glorious clouds hang in the west,
Like a pavilion of the blest,
And one bright solitary star
Is shining on the scene from far.

When the weary pilgrim wends his way
To seek his shrine at twilight gray,
There, kneeling on his altar-stone,
Devoutly prays to God alone.

Scenes like these my soul inspires
With nobler, worthier, pure desires;
For God in nature e'er doth move
My tongue to praise with hymns of love.

THE SUNSET HOUR.

What beauty beams in yonder sky,
With folding clouds of sunset die;
A pensive beauty all unknown
To every hour except its own
So Eden-like its deep repose,
We gaze, forgetful of our woes;
And while we gaze, we seem to hear
Sweet voices from a holier sphere,—
And almost catch the music tone
Which ever swelleth near the throne;
Breathings of some seraphic lyre,
And hymns by cloven tongues of fire.

Hail! white-robed dwellers of that home;
Do ye those fields of sunset roam?
And do those gaudy clouds of haze
Enveil you from my ardent gaze?

Sure heaven does never seem so dear,
Nor the departed half so near,
As at the tranquil sunset hour,
When fancy rules with potent power.

Then, back to memory's mystic cell
Returns that friend we loved so well;
The well-known form seems flitting by,
We see affection's beaming eye,
And fondly, sweetly beams it yet,
As ere the seal of death was set;
And all unconscious we extend
Our own, to grasp the friendly hand,
While half we utter words of love,
Though neither tongue nor lip does move;
We gaze upon that friend—our own,—
But soon, too soon, the vision's flown.

Ah! then we sigh for that blest time
Which shall convey us to that clime,—
The sunset of this mortal strife,
The morning of eternal life.

SUNSHINE.

'Twas in the latter part of June,
   There had been a long and drizzling rain,
And everything seemed out of tune,
   When lo! the sun broke forth again.

He rolled his heavy curtains back,
   And showed his pathway, blue and clear;
Tip'd all the distant hills with gold,
   And lit the steeples, far and near.

A moist wind sprang among the trees,
   When each began to nod to the other;
The birch shook hands with the sturdy ash,
   And the oak saluted the pine as a brother.

Then the birds came singing from the woods,
   As full of mirth as they could be;
They perched on garden-wall and gate,
   And on the top of every tree.

And sung, O such delicious notes,
   As I thought no birds e'er sung before;

While I stood list'ning, half transfixed,
    Inside the garden door.

Two little brown mates came with the rest,
    And perched on the limb of a cherry tree,
Who sung with all their might and strength
    Chick-a-dee, chick-a-dee dee dee.

A poor man came along the road,
    Who on his shoulder a huge ham bore;
And his heart was so full of joyousness
    That moment, it ran o'er.

And he sung with the birds, like a bird of Spring,
    And ere I was aware,
My own heart had leaped up to sing,
    In spite of its load of care.

And the birds sung louder,
    For they seemed to know that human hearts were gay,
And they thrilled the heart of each passing child,
    Who cheered them all along the way.

TO A RED-BREAST, SINGING.

Sweet minstrel of yon ancient grove,
   Thy notes recall the buried years,
Long ere this heart had known a grief,
   These eyes been dimmed with tears.

O who would deem a thing so small
   Had power to conjure up the past?
To make my heart beat quick and strong
   With rapture which I wish might last.

A debt, not small, to thee I owe;
   Accept what to thee doth belong;
May many blooming seasons come,
   Ere death shall hush thy song.

And may those blooming summers teem
   With fruits and flowers thou shalt approve;
And may'est thou have a downy nest,
   With winged jewels of thy love.

And may thy mate sing sweet to thee,
   Perched lordly high on some green limb,

When thou dost for awhile retire
    From all the world but him.

And be thy life one cloudless day;
    Thy bower be of the thornless rose,
Where thou may'est rest thy weary wing
    In undisturbed repose.

But should chill frosts thy bower invade,
    I fear I shall sustain a loss;
For then thou'lt fly on speedy wing
    Toward the Southern Cross.

Should'st thou find there one fettered form,
    Pray tell him this,—and more,—
"One heart at least doth bleed for him
    On our Atlantic shore."

Tell those who do the fetters bind,
    Tell with unbated breath,
That their raving's but the agony
    Which preceeds the calm of death.

Tell them the watch-fires on their hills
    Are kindled even now,
And that the sword of justice waits
    To lay their idol low.

THE MYSTERIOUS BIRD.

There's a sweet-voiced bird in the deep, dark wood,
Where the great oaks and pines have for centuries stood,
Twining their boughs in close embrace,
Making shady and cool its dwelling-place.

It comes in the leafy month of June,
When the heart with nature is most in tune,
It comes on the fragrant breath of flowers,
And each bud and leaf of the deep green bowers
Has trembled and thrilled, with its music rare,
As it gushed from the woods on the wavy air.

Sweetest it sings in the early morn,
When it mingles its notes with the hunter's horn;
Or just at night, when the balmy dew
On the tender corn falls fresh and new.

O this mystic bird, with wings so lithe,
With notes both grave, and sad, and blithe,

How oft I've listened, and held my breath,
When they seemed like the solemn dirge of death;
And then they would change to a joyous swell,
Lively and gay as a marriage-bell;
Anon, far echoing down the vale,
They would seem like a tender, mournful wail;
Then, warbling, quivering, delicious, sweet,
As if all sweet sounds in the grove did meet;
As if anointed with gladness on such days,
It pours out its heart in a gush of praise;
And I've thought that an angel might pause to hear
Its tremulous notes, so unearthly clear.

I think that Audubon hath not shown
From whence this tuneful creature hath flown;
Perhaps, from some heavenly mountain afar
It has come on a ray of some beautiful star,
For such emotions of soul its strains do impart,
It seems born of the blood of some Nymphean
    heart;
And more than once I have listened and wept
When its melting tones o'er my soul has swept,—
Swept like the wind-harp's pensive roll,
With a nameless joy beyond control.

O, indeed I love it! this sweet-voiced bird,
Which so often to rapture my spirit hath stirred,

When my heart has leaped, like the bounding roe,
Out of its deepest depths of woe ;
And evermore when it sings in its glee
'Tis a ministering spirit unto me.

This musical creature I never have seen,
But have fancied its plumage was golden and green ;
Yet when I drink in its sweet notes as they roll,
Then the bird seems to me like a white-robed soul.

Once on a lovely, calm, cool morn,
Its dulcet notes from our roof were borne ;
They came like the gush of a silver rill,
And my nerves like the chords of a lute did thrill,
And every leaf on the old roof-tree
Seemed to quiver and shake with its melody ;
But 'twas only once—no more, no more,—
That it sweetly sang o'er our vine-wreathed door,
And I strained my eyes to see its form,
But the sweet voiced creature had flown !—'twas
    gone,—
Yet I heard its melting, sweet refrain,
A short way off, o'er a field of grain.

THE WOUNDED BIRD.

[A sportsman of the canton of Mauberge has lately shot a beautiful wild pigeon, which gave another proof of how highly the instinct of animals is somctmes developed.

On plucking the bird, an old wound was discovered, over which several small leaves of plants had been carefully placed. The plumage of the bird had been so carefully arranged over it that no trace of the wound appeared.]

Beautiful bird of the wounded breast,
Thou wast out in the morn from thy cosy nest,
In quest of food for thy fledgelings dear,
When a wanton sportsman hurried near.

He aimed with cruel hand his gun,
A scream, and the shameful work is done!
A fluttering, and a mournful cry,
Fallen to the ground, but not to die.

And soon thou did'st soar on bleeding wing,
To the valley where cool waters spring;
Where thou did'st find the healing leaf,
Which gave to thy aching wound relief.

And when the healing leaf was found,
It was placed most skillful o'er the wound,
As if by some humane hand of care,—
Beautiful bird, who placed it there?

Who taught thee where grew that potent leaf,
And its virtues which brought to thee relief?
And whose was the pitying hand of care,
Or, wounded bird, did'st thou place it there?

One taught thee whose care is over all;
Who notes the little sparrow's fall;
Who every wound and grief doth see,
And cares, dear bird, for thee and me.

Oft bleeding hearts are led to find
A healing leaf, no other mind
But His who knows when to apply,
And the deep fount of sorrow dry.

TO A FRIEND, ON BEING PRESENTED WITH A BEAUTIFUL TEA-ROSE.

Dear lady of the placid brow,
   Of intellect and taste refined,
This beauteous rose, so sweet and fair,
   Is a true emblem of thy mind.

Heatly I've pressed the beauteous thing,
   Valued both for the gift and thee;
And with other rich mementoes keep,
   Which are most dear to me.

I've lain it in a casket rare,
   And there I long would let it be,
That sometimes I may view it o'er,
   With precious thoughts of thee.

May sweet flowers bloom along thy path,
   And midst them Sharon's rose be found,
The lily of the valley there*
   Forever more abound.

*"I am the rose of Sharon, and the lily of the valley."

ON VISITING DREW BROOK.

Before I reached the margin,
   Where in childhood I did tread,
I heard its laughing waters
   Above its pebbly bed.

And so I said, "I'm just thirteen,
   I'm thirteen, and no more,"
For the echo of my childhood voice
   Is dying 'long the shore.

So I took a stone from off the ground,
   And flung it on the brink,
To see how many I could count
   Before the stone would sink.

And then I sung—and tried to laugh
   As I had laughed before;
But the echo answered, cold and dull;
   It was not that of yore.

Then, seated on a crumbling log,
   Which the woodman's axe laid low,

I counted up just forty years,—
  'Twas forty years ago

That I last saw its grassy marge,
  Last heard its waters flow,
Last saw the playful, speckled trout,
  Sport midst the rocks below.

And then I thought of other years,
  When, just up yonder hill,
There stood the cottage where we lived,
  And which remaineth still.

Now stranger voices there are heard;
  Strange feet now press its floor;
And those we once did love so well
  Come not within its door.

I thought of many a sunny day,
  When, hand in hand, I'd roved,
And culled the violet and the rose,
  With playmates dearly loved.

Beside this much-loved stream I sit,
  Or wander in my sleep;
Dream of loved scenes of long ago,
  And often wake to weep.

A beauteous bird in pensive tone,
   Sung softly, sweet, and low;
It seemed the spirit of my friend,
   Who died long years ago.

And there it sung—that solemn bird,—
   As he did sing of yore,
Whose strains I ne'er can hear again
   Till heard on yonder shore.

And then I wandered far, far down
   Into the deep, dark wood,
And grieved for many a stately tree
   Which in my youth hath stood;

Stood there like giants, tall and strong,
   To guard the ancient stream.
O if I ever felt, 'twas then,
   That "life is but a dream."

Ye friends and scenes of other days,
   Will ye no more return?
And must my heart your absence grieve,
   Till it to ashes burn?

Thou spark akin to Deity!
   Spark of celestial fire!
Longing and grieving for the lost,
   Rest not on earth,—look higher!

A SONG.—THE BEAUTIFUL TREES.

Air—"Bower of Prayer."

The trees—the great trees,
   Which grow high on the hills,
And the beautiful trees,
   Which droop o'er the rills;
Lo! now in the breeze
   How they rev'rently nod,
And wave their long arms,
   As if talking of God,
   As if talking of God.

There are trees which to me
   Are most sacredly dear;
One shaded our cottage
   For many a year;
But we left that dear cottage
   A long time ago,
And its new owner's axe
   Has long since lain it low,
   Has long since lain it low.

O the old apple tree,
   I, in childhood, did prize,
Its blossoms in Spring-time,
   Delighted my eyes,
Its fruitage, in Autumn,
   Lay thick on the ground,—
But now of that tree
   Not a vestige is found,
   Not a vestige is found.

By an old mossy wall,
   Which I oft think about,
Grow a row of pomegranates
   Which grandpa set out;
In their redness and ripeness
   Shower-like they would fall,
And fill up the chinks
   In the tumble-down wall,
   In the tumble-down wall.

But my heart's dearest tree
   Was one on the homestead,
Which shaded the well
   By the door of our shed;
It was planted by her,
   Our own mother, so dear,—
But that tree and that mother,
   Alas! are not here,
   Alas! are not here.

The trees—the yew trees,
　　Which bend low o'er the dead,
And like sentinels guard
　　Their lonely green bed;
How mournful they look
　　In the moon's solemn light,
As they motionless stand
　　In the stillness of night,
　　In the stillness of night.

MY BROTHER.

Gone, gone at last!
    Dear brother of the pallid brow,
Thy weary days of suffering passed,
    Thou art an angel now.

Clothed with thine house from heaven
    Which ne'er can know decay,
Sweet blooming health to thee is given,
    Throughout eternity.

Forgive me, O my brother, now,
    That I would fain have held thee here!
That selfish wish so loth to bow,
    That sad, foreboding tear.

I knew full well, for many a year,
    That Death had set his seal on thee,
The solemn winds I oft did hear
    Moan through our family tree.

Where many a sere and yellow leaf
    Hangs shivering in the Autumn blast:

Soon, one by one, like thee, will fall,
  'Till all are gone at last.

And other eyes than ours will weep,
  To see it sere and bare,
And other hearts their vigils keep,
  When we shall not be there.

We've lain thy form where ours shall rest,
  In death's unconscious sleep;
And here thy dove, with wounded breast,
  Doth her lone vigils keep.

O dost thou know when she doth come,
  And lay her offerings here?
Those Autumn wreaths, baptized with tears,
  And twined with silent prayer.

Perchance, thy spirit ling'ring here,
  With pity, such as angels feel,
Would gently wipe the falling tear,
  The wounded bosom heal,

O God! the agony which hides
  In hearts asunder torn!
O the dark barrier which divides
  Warm hearts so loved—our own!

Saviour, through tears we look to thee,
 Thou, who the silent vale hath trod,
Thine own dear hand shall lead us through,
 Up to the mount of God.

THE WIDOWED HEART.

Widow!—how oft that word is spoken
   With careless lips and thoughtless air;
How little thought of heart that's broken,
   Of anguish-throbs that's there.

Lone watcher of a starless night,
   Beside the ever-moaning sea,
Who vainly waiting for the light
   Which comes no more to thee.

Part of thine heart is in the dust,
   While that which doth remain must bleed,
While nature claims its own, it must
   Be desolate indeed! indeed!!

I've thought of the loneliest things on earth,
   Which human form doth wear;
The loneliest things which have their birth,
   On land, or sea, or air.

A lone star on the brow of night;
   One solitary cloud at even;

AN AUTUMNAL WREATH.

A corpse shut in from every light,
   Which comes from earth or heaven.

A dweller on some dizzy height;
   A hermit on a desert isle;
The silence of an Arctic night;
   'Neath Boreal-crimson's pile.

One lone, lost mariner at night,
   Upon a vast and unknown sea,
Without a ray of hope or light,
   Is not so lone as she.

Alone, alone, amidst the throng
   Of mirth and festive glee,
Where rapturous music floats along,—
   To her 'tis mockery.

Sorrows I've seen from which my soul
   Did turn away in pain,—
Where grief broke forth beyond control,
   And sympathy was vain.

But this is not the deepest grief
   Which hearts bereft can feel,
For tears will oft, like soothing balm,
   The heart's deep sorrow heal.

The tearless, speechless agony
  Within itself, the soul, shut in,
Listening to voices of the past,
  It ne'er may hear again.

This is the sorrow-cankering rust,
  'Tis the sublimity of grief,
Which turns the widowed heart to dust,
  E'er death brings its relief.

THE LAST DAY OF SUMMER.

Thou art going, sweet Summer,—
   Just taking thy leave,—
And when thou art gone
   My spirit will grieve.

I feel thou art going,
   By many a token,
Tho' none do declare it,
   And no word is spoken.

Instinctive, mine eye
   In sadness doth turn
To the deep saffron west,
   Where thy sunset doth burn,

I have loved thee, O Summer,
   And when thou'rt away,
On the hills of the south,
   With the zephyrs at play,

I shall think of the flowers
   In my path thou hast spread,

Of the grass thou hast grown
  O'er my beautiful dead.

And tho' thou hast taken
  The delight of mine eyes,
And borne him away
  With my heart to the skies,

'Twas his joy to exchange
  The cross for the crown,—
At the close of life's march
  The staff to lay down.

O that rapturous morn!
  The blissful surprise!
When that pilgrim of earth
  Was the guest of the skies.

Take my hand now, O Summer,
  And when thou dost return,
If thou find'st me not here,
  Shed no tear on my urn.

Keep thy night-falling tears
  For the youthful and cheery;
But O waste them not
  O'er the pilgrim so weary.

I shall go where the flowers
   Are brighter in hue,—
Where no more will be spoken
   The mournful adieu.

CLOSET PRAYER.

'Tis nightfall—care and labor o'er,
Entering, I'll shut my closet door;
My secret soul into one list'ning ear
Would breathe its 'plaints where none but God can
    hear.

O Thou who once did wear the thorny crown,
Low at thy feet I lay my burden down.
What wilt thou?—Dear Christ, that I receive my
    sight,—
Anoint mine eyes that I may see aright.

Dear Lord, as with a candle, search my heart,
And make it pure and clean in every part;
Let no unholy motive even dare
To enter in, and find a lodgement there.

I seem to see, as I've not seen before,
My many failings, which I now deplore;
Rich blessings which my blindness hath not seen;
O heart of mine, how thankless thou hast been!

I come a beggar at thy footstool, Lord!
Yet not for sordid dust to basely hoard;
But for forgiving grace, thy tender love,
For daily bread which cometh from above.

For constancy, which never leaves thy fold,
And charity, all that my heart can hold;
For a pure heart which keeps the golden rule,
And loveth *all*, 'tho not of the same school.

All this, and more, I beg, O Holy One:
Nevertheless, I pray, "thy will be done;"
"Just as thou wilt," for me has e'er been best,
And in this blest assurance now I rest.

O blessed, sacred Presence! Thou art near,
And speaking to my inmost heart and ear;
O yes, it is thy answering voice divine,
Saying, "daughter, thou art ever with me, all I have is thine."

TO MY HUSBAND, ON NEW YEAR'S DAY.

"A happy New Year" thou hast wished me to-day,
   And I would that the same be thine own,—
Be they happy as those which on time's rapid wing,
   Have so happy and peacefully flown.

On the morn of our union hope gilded the scene,
   Now sweet memories light up the past;
May such memories increase with every new year,
   And gladden our lives to the last.

Embalmed in my heart is thy kindness, thy truth,
   For thy word is assurance when given,—
Ever true as the needle which points to the pole,
   Or the sun which gildeth yon heaven.

O may many new years unto thee be given,
   And may I long walk by thy side;
And when the dark river we both have crossed o'er,
   May I then be thy heavenly bride.

TO LAVINIA.

Oft I recall the blissful day,
    When first we, kindred spirits, met;
O that sweet rapture-breathing hour,
    I never, never can forget.

A vision of a home refined,
    On Androscoggin's shore,
And a sweet, mild, Madonna face,
    Doth haunt me evermore.

Give back, O time, that distant day,
    Of soul-enlivening mirth;
And let me feel again the warmth
    Of that dear genial hearth;

Where plants and flowers, and books, and shells,
    Pure taste, and love had made
A lonely Paradise on earth,
    Where angels sometimes strayed.

'Twas there the sense informed the soul,
    The eye met beauty everywhere,

And voices, sweet as silver lutes,
    Fell on the perfumed air.

How oft I think of thee, — of once,
    When, hand in hand, one night,
We wandered by a river-side,
    Beneath the moon's pale light.

Of that sweet, pensive evening hour,
    When the holy stars looked out,
When day's last parting gleam had died,
    And angels were about.

The dew fell not more soothing, sweet,
    Upon the waiting flower,
Than the sweet influence of the scene
    Upon our hearts, that hour.

'Twas where the flood-tides of the spring
    Had washed the vernal sod;
'Neath heaven's high vault of blue and gold,
    We stood and thought of God.

In early youth, in tender years,
    Thine head with Zion's dew was wet,
And peace a heavenly coronal
    On thy fair brow was set,

Ere thy young heart had learned to pour
   Its ecstasies in song,
That heart was on God's altar laid,—
   Laid where it did belong.

And oft when night her curtain weaves,
   And flings it o'er the day,
I think at this hushed, hallowed hour,
   Lavinia now doth pray.

Retired within her cloistered room,
   In audience with her God,
She prays for strength to walk the road
   The world's Redeemer trod.

My heart grieves that we're far apart;
   It may no more be given
On earth our friendship to renew,
   But sweet 'twill be in heaven.

TO OCTAVIA.

Thou wast the nursling of our fold,
    The lambkin of our flock,
The birdling of the downy nest,
    A sweet flower on our stalk.

I was a child when thou wast sent
    To bless our quiet home;
I took thee to my heart of hearts,
    Rejoiced that thou hadst come.

In thy budding life how we did love
    To kiss thy lily-velvet cheek,
To look into thy baby eyes,
    So blue, so saintly meek.

Long years have past; thy matron form
    Grief and disease have rung,
And o'er the lustre of thine eye
    Their pensive shades have flung.

My heart is sorely pained for thee,
    Thou patient, suffering one!

I've seen on thy once blooming cheek
  What dire disease hath done.

Fain would I clasp thee to my heart,
  And ward off every pain,
Again revive thy cherished hopes
  Which long in dust have lain.

Grieve not for me, thou stricken one,
  That I in weakness pine;
A few more weary steps, and I
  Shall go to a healthier clime.

I've had my share of joy and health,
  And now I cannot long abide;
Tho' strong the ties which bind me here,
  My treasure's on the other side.

TO CARRIE.

O how we miss thee, Carrie! come,
    Come back to us again!
We miss thee as the tender grass
    Misses the April rain.

We miss thee as the lonesome bird
    Misses its absent mate,
When its nest hangs cheerless, high, and cold,
    Forsaken, desolate.

We miss thy cheering footstep, now,
    Upon our entry floor;
And since we've lain our dead away,
    We miss thee more and more.

We miss thee at our frugal board,
    And round our social hearth;
We miss thy converse, miss thy smile,
    Thy laugh-provoking mirth;

We miss thy sympathic tear,
    Thy counsel, ever true;

And when our hearts are pained with grief,
How oft we think of you.

They miss thee in God's temple,
In His holy house of prayer;
The children miss thee in their school,—
We miss thee everywhere.

LINES.

Were all the hearts that lie
    Buried beneath the ground,
Laid bare to human sight,
    How many would be found
    With broken strings,

Which like some fine-strung lyre,
Upon whose quivering wire,
Some rude hand long hath swept,
And sorrowing eyes have wept,
Till long since lain away,
    Where oblivion o'er them crept.

HOPE.

Hope, thou art a sort of syren,
    And yet, we would not live
One single day without thee,
    For all that earth could give.

We love anticipation,
    We ever best enjoy
The good which is in prospect,—
    'Tis free from base alloy.

No disappointments linger
    Around expectant bliss;
We ever reckon with our host
    For joy, and nothing less.

But when the pleasure cometh,
    It is a mingled cup,
Devoid of half its sweetness,
    Yet we must drink it up.

And ever doth Hope whisper
    I have riches, joys in store;

So we live ever hoping, —
Just this and nothing more.

But there will come a time,
When hope shall be fruition,
In a clime awaiting us,
The sweet, the bright Elysium.

TO ONE BELOVED.

O friend beloved! thou tried and true,
    I've found thee evermore the same,
With willing ear and heart to lend,
    Whene'er affliction came.

I've known thee long and loved thee well,—
    In health my heart was knit to thine;
Yet *close* and *stronger* are the ties,
    Since I in illness pine.

Regardless of thy weal or woe,
    Unmindful of thy needful rest,
Thy tender, sympathetic heart,
    In blessing others is most blest.

How suffering ones crave sympathy,
    How pine and languish where not found;
Then droop and die like tender flowers
    On uncongenial ground.

As doth the dove, with wounded breast,
    Press to its mate its bleeding wing,

So round loved souls do I in pain
    More close and fondly cling.

There's healing in a friendly hand,
    When pressed upon the aching head,
And music in affection's voice
    Breathed low around the sufferer's bed.

And when a tearful, loving eye,
    In pity o'er our sufferings bend,
It seems like the sweet healing balm,
    Heaven doth sometime in mercy send.

Sorrow, dear friend, has been our lot,
    And to the dregs we've drained its cup;
Yet, fainting, turned we not away,—
    Heaven gave us strength to drink it up.

Adversity's the golden key
    Which doth unlock life's secret springs;
It doth lay bare the inner shrine,
    Disclosing its divinest things.

O friend beloved! One at thy side,
    Who ever doth thy being guard,
For all thy patient works of love,
    Will give a rich reward.

O may the remnant of thy days
    Be free from all vexatious ills;
And may the sunset of thy life
    Be bright upon the western hills.

A SONG.—THE HERMIT.

Air—"Bower of Prayer."

Down in a sweet vale
   Where the coney doth hide,
And the willows bend low,
   Where a brooklet doth glide,
A lone hermit dwelt,
   That clear streamlet beside,
For many sad years,
   Since his Mary had died,
   Since his Mary had died.

His heart's passion flower
   He had left o'er the sea,
Pale, withered, and dead,
   Neath the dark cypress tree.
And when hope in his bosom
   No longer did burn,
Across the wide waters
   His lone heart did turn,
   His lone heart did turn.

On the banks of a stream
   He built him a shed,
And with flowers of the forest
   He made him a bed.
His rude table was hewn
   From the heart of a tree,
And laden with books,
     And rare shells from the sea,
     And rare shells from the sea.

He would roam o'er the hills,
   'Neath the dark forest trees,
And listen to voices
   Which came on the breeze;
When he'd answer a voice
   Which he oft seemed to hear,
Like the voice of his lost one
   It seemed to his ear,
   It seemed to his ear.

When low in the west
   The red sunset did burn,
Lone, weary, and sad,
   To his cabin he'd turn;
With his flute and his books,
   Where none oft did intrude,
He pass'd the lone twilight
   In deep solitude,
   In deep solitude.

In recalling the past,
　　When his Mary did glide
Like a beautiful fawn
　　Ever close by his side.
And here he'd live over
　　And over again,
In memory, the hours,
　　Ere his life-star did wane,
　　Ere his life-star did wane.

A bracelet of gold,
　　And a ringlet of hair,
Near his sorrowing heart
　　He forever did wear;
And when death had lain him
　　Beside the cold stream,
He looked like a saint
　　In a sorrowful dream,
　　In a sorrowful dream.

Close pressed to his heart
　　Was that lock of brown hair,
And the bracelet of gold,
　　Which his young bride did wear.
There kind friends did bury him,
　　Afar from his home,
No more a lone hermit,
　　In sadness to roam,
　　In sadness to roam.

TO THE GREAT SEA.

Agent of Heaven!
   Awful! sublime!
Roll on in thy grandeur,
   Twin-brother of time!

Smooth down thy white mane,
   So tangled and torn
By rough breakers and boulders,
   Since creation was born.

Mysterious art thou,
   In thine ebb and thy flow;
Dost ascend to the zenith,
   Then tumble below.

Great highway of nations,
   Dispenser of health,
Deep hid in thy bosom
   Is earth's choicest wealth.

Huge continents, down
   In thy fathomless deep,

Lie maturing for earth,
   In their embryo sleep,

Where for ages they've lain,
   And blinked to the sun
As other continents did,
   When time first begun.

Leviathans sport
   And play at their base,
Like lambs on the hills
   When they gambol and race.

And the swift dolphin leaps,
   Where the sea-flowers bloom,
In thy gardens of coral,
   Where the sea-nymphs come.

Thou dost mirror the heavens
   With their glittering host,
The isles with their mountains,
   And the illimitable coasts.

And Miriam's song
   Is still echoed o'er thee,
By thy sweet-voiced shells,
   O musical sea!

From the fount of the eternal
   Thy billows do spring;
He taketh thee up,
   As a very small thing.

He appointeth thy bounds,
   Which forever must stand;
For His *will* is the barrier
   Twixt thee and the land.

From the palm of his hand
   He poureth thee out;
The moring stars saw thee,
   And sent forth a shout;

And the infantile world
   Joined in accord,
In lisping their praise
   To the infinite Lord.

The loud-voiced thunders
   Do roll over thee,
And thou foamest in wrath,
   O terrible sea!

And the red lightnings flash
   O'er thy wreck-strewn path;
Yet thou laugh'st them to scorn,
   In thy fury and wrath.

Woe, woe to the man
  Who'd make fetters for thee!—
What consummate folly
  Such weakness must be!

With one sigh from thy heart
  Thou wouldst blow out his breath;
With one wave of thy wand
  Thou wouldst fling him to death.

Yet a pathway is made
  Through thy vastness immense;
A high-way for thought,—
  More subtle than sense.

And distance and time,
  How standeth aghast,
To find they're subdued
  And conquered at last.

And the great heart of nations
  Is brought nigh and nigher,
As thoughts breathe and burn
  O'er the 'lectrical wire,

And peace and good-will
  Is breathed though thy caves,
Far down, down, beneath
  Thy deep heaving waves.

We are awed by thy greatness,
   Stupendous sea;
In the scale of creation
   What pigmies are we.

Our days fly like chaff,
   Our life is a span;
Yet eternal art thou
   Compared with man.

Proud nations have vanished
   Who lived by thy side;
And kings, with their subjects,
   Midst centuries have died.

Yet thou are the same,
   And ever will be;
Till the word goeth forth,
   "There shall be no more sea."

Yet our spirits, immortal,
   Eternal, sublime,
Shall survive o'er the wreck
   Of all objects of time.

And the trembler, now,
   Who stands humbled by thee,
Shall outlive thy greatness,
   O perishable sea!

THE DROUGHT.

Ah me! the blessed rain,
No longer on the window pane,
    Is running down:
But oh! the burning sun
Leaves his heat, when day is done,
    On our frame.

There is not a friendly cloud
Our aching heads to shroud
    From his rays:
And nothing can we see
But parched-up flower and tree,
    'Midst smoke and haze.

The scanty water's hot
Before it's in the pot,
    O'er the fire;
And still the heat pours in,
And so parches up the skin
    It can't perspire.

The poor farmer, all athirst,
With his eyes so full of dust
    He scare can see,
Hoes his withered corn,
And each dryer, hotter morn,
    Wonders what 'twill be.

Ah! I see beneath his brow,
As his head is bending low
    O'er his breast;
An anxious, watchful eye,
Which turns toward the sky
    In the West.

In hope he ploughed and sow'd,
And cheerfully he hoed,
    All the Spring,
And now he looks forlorn,
For his hope, as well as corn,
    Is withering.

The cattle on the hills,
Just beyond the silent mills,
    Low for rain,
And run, moaning, through the glen,
Far from the haunts of men,
    In burning pain.

And the birds have flown away,
So we hear no more their lay
   'Midst the flowers,
They have flown on weary wing
Where gushing waters spring
   In shady bowers.

The poor old mottled duck
Is struggling in the muck,
   Trying to swim;
O, for a little flood,
To wash away the mud
   Which cleaves to him.

And still, each sun's return,
Threatens the world to burn;
   And we all
Pray the meek prophet's prayer;
Thou God of mercy hear
   While we call.

But still, one burning glare
Above, and everywhere
   Meets the eye,
And we hear no more the mill,
The river's voice is still,—
   It is dry.

A strangeness gathers here,
And all things seem to wear
    A gloomy hue,
There's no clear setting sun,
When the scorching day is done,
    Nor healing dew.

Ah me! the burning drought,
Come, moist wind from the South,
    O hither come.
Come, then, O blessed rain!
Run down the window-pane,—
    Hark! it has come.

TO L——E.

[Suggested by reading one of his poems.]

Why covet wings to fly,
   Thou of the winged lyre?—
The deep-toned music of thy notes
   Seem fraught with living fire.

Could I but soar as thou dost soar,
   And sing as thou dost sing,
I'd ask no seraph's wing to bear
   Me back from whence we spring;

For earth would seem a heaven indeed,
   And every stone and tree
Would echo with the mystic strains
   Borne down from heaven to me.

Could I but pour my soul in song,
   Like thee when thou dost sing,
I'd ask not for the speed of light,
   Or flash of lightning's wing.

Thy melting strains, ere thou didst roam
  In Palestine awhile,
Are lingering with me evermore,
  Borne from thy blooming isle.

Before thou, in the "desert-bark,"
  Had sailed o'er seas of sand,
Or in the Jordan, dark and cool,
  Had bathed thy burning hand,—

Ere thy glad feet did stand
  Where David fed his flock,
Or where the water, cool and sweet,
  Gushed from the flinty rock,—

Where flamed the burning bush,—
  Where gleamed the Eden-sword,—
Where Sinai, thro' the fire and smoke,
  Beheld creation's Lord,—

And then didst walk o'er Bethlehem's height,
  Where shepherd's watched their sheep,
Stood where the sorrowing prophet stood,
  Who hushed his lyre to weep,—

The dark, sad mount of sacrifice
  Did'st see with tearful eye,

And heard in ruined Ninevah
  The jackal's mournful cry,—

With reverent soul didst kneel
  Low at the Saviour's shrine,
And wept such tears as none can weep
  But souls akin to thine.

God's ministers, like living flame,
  Do all thy being scan,
And in thine aspirations high,
  Discern the angel in the man.

God hears the beating of thine heart,—
  Hath warmed it with a pure desire;
And from the altar near his throne
  Hath touched thy lips with hallowed fire.

Thine heart is pillowed on His breast,
  And camped about thee is His host,
Who evermore do watch and guard
  The temples of the Holy Ghost.

For height, nor depth, nor life, nor death,
  Can thee from Him divide;
For, as in Eden's dewy dawn,
  He walketh by his children's side.

And evermore along our paths
  Come rapture-breathing strains,
Which my dull ear may never catch
  While camped on earthly plains.

Ah, would that ere I taste of death,
  My spirit, like thine own,
Might bathe in that pure fount divine,
  Which flows from 'neath the throne.

THE RESURRECTED HARP.

["Recently, an Egytian harp has been disentombed in Thebes, with its strings yet perfect enough to vibrate after a silence of three thousand years."]

Unveiled thy silent form at last,
   Harp of the ancient years!
Thy quivering strings awake again,
   But gone the Orient seers.

Long ere th' angelic strains were heard
   O'er Bethlehem's star-lit hills,
The echo of whose heaven-fraught notes
   The world's deep bosom fills,

Thou didst sleep in the depths of thy cloistered cell,
   While centuries were marching by,—
Hid 'neath the tramp of proud nations gone,
   Who live in eternity.

Who now, perhaps, in melting strains,
   High on the heavenly hills,

Chant to the lyre the thrilling note
   Which heaven with rapture fills.

Perhaps the weeping prophet's wail
   Has woke thy quivering strings,—
Sounding the deepest founts of grief,
   Stirring their hidden springs.

Did not some gentle Hebrew maid
   Sit at the Syrian's feet, —
Or some tall, proud, Egyptian dame
   Lessons on thee repeat?

The sweetest strains which Syria taught
   May oft have thrilled thy wires,
'Midst Egypt's chieftains,—her proud sons,—
   And her gray-bearded sires.

Swept were thy chords by cunning hands;
   Thy strains were wafted in the air,
Laden, sometimes, with burning sighs,
   Or freighted deep with prayer,—

Kindled devotion's smouldering fires,
   And raised her drooping wings,
Or soothed the dying in the vale,
   Or calmed the rage of kings,—

Or breathed the soul of tranquil rest,
  Caused discord dire to cease,
Where grief, the smitten heart opprest,
  Brought calm, submissive peace.

Hail to thee, resurrected harp!
  Whose years are now renewed;
Yet thou must mourn in fitful strains,
  Thy long, dark solitude.

No psalm of praise swept o'er thy chords
  On Jesus' natal morn,
Or breathed of heaven's impartial love,
  When He, the Christ, was born.

UNWRITTEN MUSIC.

'Tis said that an old philosopher,
    With spirit most devout,
Discerned that the skies were all writ o'er,
    Within and roundabout,

With notes of music, and the stars
    Moved on, as in a merry dance,
And all the joyous shining things
    Seemed in a blissful trance.

But yet, there was not harmony,—
    Two stars were wanting to fill the chime,
And he pointed out the vacant space
    Where two bright stars appeared in time.

But the good old man has gone to his home,—
    He saw them not from this mortal shore;
Yet who knows but he saw from his seat of bliss,
    And heard the notes once more.

We have heard that in the Highlands,
    Where the simple soul sees God,

That they bear their dying from the house
   And lay them on the sod.

And there, just out from the shieling,
   Beneath the clear blue sky,
Drinking in ecstatic music,
   They calmly, sweetly die.

They say that the senses are quickened,
   When death is drawing near,
And that most delicious music
   Is heard by the dying ear,—

That the eye beholds such glories
   As they've never seen before;
And, enraptured, they gaze on the beautiful scenes,
   They are soon to behold no more.

There is sweet, unwritten music
   Above and all around,—
There is music in the seedlings,
   As they sprout beneath the ground.

In our simple love of nature,
   We have lain our ear to the sod,
And heard the springing blades of grass
   Whispering the praise of God.

The sap doth know its time
   To ascend into the limbs,
And it creepeth, softly singing
   Its low, sweet, vernal hymns.

The little yellow catkins
   Beside the singing brook,
And the crispy, early cowslip
   In the moist and shady nook,

Whisper unwritten music,
   As the breeze goes singing by,
Guided by a hand divine,
   Watched by the Omnicient eye.

From the remote eternities,
   Infinite space has thrilled,
With sweet, unwritten music,
   And our list'ning earth been filled.

And its great heart hath moved,
   And its deep pulse hath beat,
And we have heard the sound thereof
   In the tramp of the earthquake's feet.

And yet the *grandest* music
   Is down in the depths of the soul,

When the eye surveys the heavens,
  Where worlds in order roll.

Then the *sweetest* of all music
  In the glow of filial love,
Hymneth, "Abba, Father,"
  When lip nor tongue doth move.

IN WAR TIME.

Sheathe, sheathe thy sword, O death!
   Foul fiend of war, forbear!
Thy breath is hot with wrath and hate,
   And blood flows everywhere.

From wounded hearts at home,
   Blood flows as red and warm
As ever flowed on the field of death,
   Amidst the leaden storm.

In the dark dead of night,
   Mothers and children weep
For fathers on the gory field,—
   Perhaps in their last sleep.

Not only on the field of strife,
   Where death-shells rattle by,
But daily in our darkened homes
   Do freedom's martyrs die.

From all her bleeding wounds
   Our country cried for peace;

Lord, lay thine hand upon her heart,
    And bid its throbbing cease!

Our brothers groan in chains,
    By vile oppression cursed,
And our proud banner, so beloved,
    Is trailing in the dust.

Arm of the Lord, awake!
    Arise, and pity them!
The sons of Ham are in thy sight
    As dear as pale-faced Shem.

We care not where they had their birth,
    Nor what their pedigree;
It is enough for us to know
    They pine for liberty.

If more blood must be shed
    This crime to wash away,
Help us, while we in sackcloth grieve,
    To work, and wait, and pray:

Pray for thine own good time,
    For thou the word hath spoke;
Thou wilt unloose each galling chain,
    And break the captive's yoke.

Then righteousness shall bloom
 On every land and sea,
And Ethiop, from her sea-girt isles,
 Stretch out her hands to Thee.

DEATH OF OUR MARTYRED PRESIDENT.

"A great man hath fallen in Israel."

Toll, mournful bells, toll on;
   And if strong men weep they are forgiven,
For they weep as none e'er wept before
   For a hero gone to heaven.

Our heart of hearts, like muffled drums,
   Beat strangly heavy, faint, and low,
While mourners throng the silent streets,
   In sable garbs of woe.

The burdened air is full of sighs,
   The nation-soul is in eclipse,
While grief, too deep for utterance,
   With silence seals our lips.

Brave compeers! how your hearts have burned,
   As ye walked with him the Emmaus road,
From which his spirit did ascend
   To his and to your God.

For ye had hoped and prayed
   That he of the noble, honest heart,
Just crowned with the palm of victory,
   Might not soon hence depart.

With wounded breast against the thorn,
   Trembling we take the bitter cup;
This is our wormwood mixed with gall,—
   Shall we not meekly drink it up?

Thou God who notes the sparrow's fall,
   Who counts the hairs upon our head,
From step to step hath led him on,
   And watched above his bloody bed.

Devoutly thankful, Lord, we feel
   For every breath of life he drew;
For on our country's bleeding cause
   His life has been a healing dew.

Heart of its heart, soul of its soul!
   Our royal pulse beat time with thine,
And, from our very being's depths,
   We hail thee as almost divine.

We gaze beyond the blue remote,
   Where thou, with martyrs gone above,
Art bending o'er our agony,
   And cheering on the cause we love.

Sad orphanage! Our God, we feel
　　So strangely, painfully bereft;
Hide us, O Rock of Ages, hide
　　Within thy sheltering cleft.
And on a true anointed head
　　Be our Elijah's mantle spread.

And when, in the distant years,
　　Our eyes with age are dim,
We shall know the place of his sepulchre,
　　For we have buried him

Where pilgrim feet will roam,
　　And Freedman's sons repair,
Unto that holy blessed shrine,
　　And pay their offerings there:

A shrine made holy by the seal
　　Of more than patriot blood;
Sacred to truth and liberty,
　　To justice, and to God.

He filled a page which fills the world,
　　And coming centuries shall bloom
With Olive-wreaths in other climes,
　　O'er hated Slavery's tomb.

Now to your tents, O Israel! fly,
　　And 'tho your chief and leader fall,

Sheath not the sword 'till traitors die,
   And right and justice's given to all.

For still the nation's heart is strong,
   Deep, deeply smitten, yet not broke;
For the broad shield of freedom gleams
   From out the fire and smoke.

'Tis done, 'tis done! sin's direst hate
   Unseals the mystery of blood,—
All o'er the mournful scroll we trace
   Bright prophecies of coming good.

Now liberty forever live!
   Thy fount of baptism, filled with blood,
Invests thee with a holier name,
   Bright with the seal of God.

Great Author of earth's destiny,
   We bow our heads unto the dust;
Nothing but good can come from thee,
   And in thy righteousness we trust.

THE SLAVE MOTHER'S LAMENT.

List, list! the low wail
   From the fair field of canes,—
How plaintive it sounds,—
   'Tis the mother complains.

They have torn from her bosom
   Her fond boy away,
And now, moaning, she toils
   Through the hot, sultry day,

Tho' the orange tree shed
   Its sweet fragrance around,
What boots it to me,
   Who in slavery bound,

Have toiled for the bread
   Which I've mingled with tears,
Since torn from my home
   In life's sunny years.

O had I the wing
   Of an eagle, I'd soar

And fly to my boy,
   Tho' to earth's farthest shore.

In the dark mountain fastness
   My home I'd prepare;
The slave-driver and hound,
   Would they ever come there?

O my boy! how he wiped the hot tears
   From these dim, weeping eyes,
While weary and sick,
   'Neath the fierce, glowing skies,

Where I've toiled, and toiled on,
   Till the evening twilight
Was veiled by the dark
   Misty curtain of night.

How he lighted my toil,
   That dear loving boy!
But he's gone from me now,—
   My heart's dearest joy.

O my heart! how it ached,
   My fast-throbbing heart,
When I saw that dear form
   Forever depart.

How closely he clung
  To my side all that day;
But my master had sold him;
  They tore him away.

My full heart, how it aches,
  My fast-throbbing heart,—
Shall I see him no more?—
  Lord why did we part?

Why did I not follow,
  Wherever he went,
Even down to the shades,
  If there he were sent?

'Midst the canes I shall die,
  'Neath the hot, sultry skies,
And no darling child
  Shall close up my eyes.

The slaver will come,
  With a heart hard as steel;
For poor bondmen in chains
  He no pity can feel.

Perhaps he'll not deem
  That my spirit's away,
And he'll lash with his whip
  My cold, sable clay.

AN AUTUMNAL WREATH.

And then he, perhaps,
   By the moon's pale light,
Will bury me up
   In some hole, out of sight.

O God of the bondman!
   Give ear to her prayer,
Ere that dark eye is fixed
   In the gaze of despair.

O may it like incense
   Which from altars doth rise,
While the warm victim smokes
   In the pure sacrifice,

Come up to thy throne,
   And acceptance there find,
Waxing mighty and mightier,
   The slave to unbind.

Till the last chain is broken,
   Thine image roams free,
And all heaven rejoices
   In the grand jubilee.

THE DEATH OF LINCOLN.

Eve in the west! how calm and mild
   The sun retires beyond the hills!
All, all unconscious of the grief
   A nation's bosom fills.

Thou hast not seen, retiring sun,
   In all thy course, so vast and wide,
A crime so dark, so deadly vile,
   Since Calvery shook, when Jesus died.

How much of goodness left the world
   When this black deed was done!
Love, tender as was that which cried,
   " Mother, behold thy son!"

Thou Judas, who the crime hath done,
   Remorse, the vulture at thine heart,
His bloody beak has buried there,
   To nevermore depart.

The eternities, while sweeping by,
   Can ne'er thy guilt efface;

Yet God, at length, in his own time,
   May give thee pardoning grace.

Treason and hate have done their worst,
   And Lincoln fills a bloody grave;
That blood calls to us from the ground,
   Almost Omnipotent to save.

Our Lincoln dead! — no, no, not dead!
   He was too good and great to die;
His God has but enlarged his sphere,
   To work for wronged humanity.

His works are here, and patriots will
   His god-like deeds repeat,
Till time shall fold his weary wing,
   And earth's last pulse shall beat.

AN EMBLEM.

One morn, with illness sore oppress'd,
   And lowly bowed with recent grief,
Weary with watching for the dawn
   Of some blest day to bring relief,

Within my dimly-lighted room
   A favorite flower, a daphne, grew,
And 'neath its fragrant parent stems
   A pale dead leaf there met my view.

I scanned the faded thing awhile,
   Which on the floor in ruin lay,
Received the ministry it gave
   Of life reviving from decay.

A power seemed near unto my heart
   Which smote the rock whence flowed a rill;
A voice said, "Wait a little while,
   New life shall yet thy being fill."

"Rise! shake the dust of suffering years
   From off thy pilgrim feet;
When thou no more to dust allied,
   Thoughts of these painful years, how sweet."

CALL ME NOT BACK.

Ye mystic powers, call me not back
   My aching head to rest
Upon the fond paternal lap,
   Or the maternal breast.

The soul, outgrown its swatheing clothes,
   Can them no longer wear,
Nor find amidst its baby-toys,
   The joy it then did share.

My hands have grown too strong to play
   With pebbles, culled on childhood's shore;
The laughing joy they gave me then
   Comes not again forevermere.

Ah, no! I would not thence return
   O'er life's long-beaten track;
Ye watchful ones who guard my life,
   O do not call me back.

I would not give these silvery hairs
   For childhood's locks of gold,

More than its tender heart of love
My older heart doth hold.

Sweet memories I have laid away,
    A casket full and running o'er;
In every little nook a gem,
    And who can ask for more?

Rich hopes hang clustering on life's tree
    Which childhood could not know;
So on from life's meridian line,
    Advancing, I would go.

I've proved the love of God to man,
    Like a clear ocean, vast and deep,
And oft beneath his shadowing palm,
    With chastened joy I weep.

Infancy, childhood, youth, are past,
    Yet brighter gleams the onward track;
Rich autumn fruits I'm gathering up,
    And I would not go back.

While from the calm, high noon of life,
    I look through time that's yet to be,
Dimly I see the shadows pass,
    And light gleam from eternity.

My harvest-noon shines clear and bright;
  O may hope's rainbow span my even,
And the mild light of Bethlehem's star
  Illume my path to heaven.

TO THE ORIOLE.

Just come from the south, pretty oriole? how
Do they do, since they've learned to justice to bow:
Since the lash and the block are things of the past,
And freedom and right have triumphed at last?

O beautiful bird! a welcome to thee,
Our yard, and our garden, and housetop are free;
Come to the cherry-tree, beautiful, come,
Here build thee a nest, and make it thy home.

To the cherries, as red as the down on thy wing,
To the strawberries, and currants, thy young
    birdies bring,
To the walk and the bower, to the fruit of each
    tree,
Thou art just as welcome as welcome can be.

O how I delight in the flash of thy wing,
And thy sweet, pensive notes, 'midst the greenness
    of spring,
When the air is all balm, and the woods full of
    song,
Then the memories of youth come trooping along.

Then, in fancy, I go to the woods, as of old,
When my life was as full of joy as't could hold;
It was then that I heard thy ancestor's lay,—
'Twas the very same song thou art singing to-day.

O sing it, dear bird, for now doth return
The sweet dream of hope with which my young heart did burn,
When my step was as light as thy wing, and as free,
And my song was as cheerful as thine e'er can be.

Dear bird, go not back where the color of skin
Has made such a fuss, such a terrible din;
Stay where the blackbirds and white sing gaily together,
And none are despised for the hue of the feather.

IN AFFLICTION.

I am sitting in the shadow
  Of a dark, a deep unrest;
Darkly it falls around me,
  And my spirit's sore opprest.

But I hear a meek voice, saying,
  "Arise, let us go hence,"
And hopefully I look and list,
  For it comes, I know from whence.

"Arise, let us go hence,"
  Let me follow where it leads;
A heart once pierced for human woes,
  For human woe still bleeds.

O blessed voice, come nearer!
  May I hear it nearer still,
And rest my human heart on thee,
  And suffer all thy will.

O yes, I'd pray, "thy will be done,"
  Not that my chastening cease,

But ask that in my troubled heart
  May be submissive peace.

Pleasant indeed has been to me
  The patient sufferer dear,
And painful now 'tis to repress
  Nature's outgushing tear.

The soul may be needed now above,
  In suffering be growing its wings;
In heaven a harp may be waiting
  For a hand to touch its strings.

The reaping angel thrice has passed
  The lintel of our door,
And yet his footsteps linger still
  Upon the threshing floor.

One we laid away in summer,
  When the lilies were in blow;
But O how sad it seems to me
  To lay one under the snow!

O precious Christ, be near
  To roll the stone away!
O angel of the covenant, guard
  The silent, sleeping clay!

Saviour, thy blessed mansions pure,
I know not where they are;
I only know that sin and death
Can never enter there.

THE GOOD SHEPHERD.

Israel's kind shepherd guards the sheep
   Within his sheltering fold:
The lambs upon his breast he bears,
   And gently leads the old.

Beside still waters, sweet and cool,
   He leads his trusting flock,
And when the noontide pour its heat,
   They rest beside the rock.

A stranger's voice they will not heed,
   Nor answer to his call;
They know that near their shepherd's side
   No danger can befall.

And in the darkness of the night
   His watchful eye doth keep;
For He who guardeth Israel's hosts
   Doth never, never sleep.

O thou my soul! take shelter here,
   Within this safe retreat;
Safe thou wilt be thro' all life's storms,—
   Safe when death's billows beat.

IN MEMORIAM.

Ah me! how much within us dies
    When our loved friends depart!
How much goes with them to the skies,
    Of our poor human heart.

Daily the heart new tendrils shoots,
    For time each friend endears;
And O how sad when death uproots
    The sturdy growth of years!

I followed one, on bleeding feet,
    Down to the river, dark and still:
There cried, while faint my heart did beat,
    "Abide with us, the night is chill."

"Abide with us,— our household hearth,
    Which thou so oft hath warmed and cheered,
Is now the loneliest place on earth,
    For there no more thy voice is heard."

A paleness overspread his face;
    The hand I held was icy cold;

As he unclasped that fond embrace,
   My soul did lose its hold.

Just then dropped down the parting veil,
   And hid him from my mournful gaze;
Yet through it came no voice of wail,
   But O such notes of praise.

And then I tried to grieve no more;
   I knew my brother had not died,
But had just crossed with the boatman o'er,
   On to the other side.

This cherished faith, like healing dew,
   Or the soft south wind's breath,
Doth an immortal hope renew;
   'Tis budding life from death.

So now I strive to dry each tear,—
   This place to me is hallowed ground;
God's covenant angel has been here,
   And my beloved has crowned.

Now, patient, by the silent stream,
   I wait the boatman's oar;
For I shall see his pale light gleam
   When he comes to take *me* o'er.

When I catch a glimpse of a pale, fair hand,
    Holding a snow-white wreath,
I shall know that wreath did blossom here,
    Amidst thy frosts, O Death.

Like the homesick mariner at night,
    When he hears the sea-bird call,
I shall rejoice to see that fadeless light,
    Where no earthly shadows fall.

LINES.

[Suggested by seeing a picture of our immortal Washington, placing the victor-wreath upon the head of our martyred Lincoln.]

Loved, sainted forms!
With reverent awe and deep surprise,
I gaze into your holy eyes,
And think of heaven's mysterious power,
Which transformed saints to seraphim,
Who chant deep, sacred, solemn hymns,
Amidst rejoicing cherubim,—
Where breathing, quivering harps scarce heard
Between profoundest silences,—
Where raptured spirits glow and burn
With ever-blissful ecstasies,—
Where holy eyes meet eyes as holy quite,
Amidst the throng who walk with Christ in white.

Our country's sire, loved Washington!
'Tis meet that thou should'st crown its son;
What hand, but thine, should place the wreath
Upon his brow who gave his breath,
A sacrifice to slavery's death?—

Apostle, priest of heaven's just laws,
He died a martyr to its cause.

The ground seems hallowed where he trod;
And if I worshipped aught but God,
Incense would from my heart arise,
While heavenward oft I turn my eyes
To bless the patriot in the skies;
And while such thoughts my soul doth lift,
I praise the giver of the gift.

Lincoln, bright soul of heavenly birth!
A hand unseen led thee on earth.
Tho' in no ark upon the sacred Nile,
Wast thou preserved from bitter death awhile,
Yet heard a voice from out the burning bush,
Saw from the smitten rock the waters gush.

From the deep billowy sea's eternal roar,—
From the bland zephyr sighing 'long its shore,—
From sun-lit hills, and from the cane-brakes low,—
From the tall palm tops, waving to and fro,—
Thou heard'st a voice. "O, let my people go."

Deep thou didst feel the burning words,
Assumed the awful trust
To raise the down-trod millions from the dust;

Yet paused awhile beside the sea of blood,
To hear and to obey the voice of God;
Then, with the covenant-ark just on before,
Thou led'st them forth, to be enslaved no more.

Twin-souls who fought for liberty and right,
Who saw the eternal morn 'merge from the night,
Bright, fadeless chaplets for your brows are made,
Millions of hearts upon your shrines are laid,
And deathless honors to your memories paid;
And nations yet unborn, will proudly vie
To bless your names, beloved, which ne'er can die.

WHAT YE KNOW NOT NOW, YE SHALL KNOW HEREAFTER.

O words breathed warm from lips divine,
    How precious the assurance given,
That what we may not know while here,
    Will be revealed in heaven.

Blest promise sweet, O let me bind
    Thee as a signet to my breast,
That in some agonizing hour,
    My heart on thee may rest,

And, patient, drink the bitter draught,
    When to the lips 'tis borne;
Know all is love, tho' darkly dressed,
    Even the wounding thorn

I look out on God's great domain,
    See truth with error strangely wed,
And walk with pained feet the ground
    Where innocence has bled.

And in my blindness grope to find
    The cause of latent ill,
And question fearful agencies
    About the Infinite will.

O Christ-like soul! still suffer on,
    And bear thy burdens, big with fate;
Life's mysteries all will be made plain,
    In the hereafter, soon or late.

And thou shalt know why blood, like sweat,
    From Christ's meek face did flow;
Why evil, evermore, was made,
    Which shrouds the world in woe.

Why death its human harvest reaps,
    Why war's red sword is bared,
Why liberty doth fail and fall,
    While tyranny is spared.

Why the pure-hearted, whom we love,
    Do die untimely young,
While guilt-stained age doth still live on
    To curse the world with wrong.

Why kindred souls are severed here,
    While uncongenial ones abound,

As thick as sands on ocean shore,
  Or grass upon the ground.

Why burdens on the weak are laid,
  Which strong ones may not bear;
Why timid souls triumph at last,
  Where valor doth despair.

Why pale disease doth wear and waste,
  And bend the high-wrought spirit down,—
Perhaps that such, through grief and pain,
  Weave an immortal, burning crown.

MY MOTHER'S GRAVE.

Solemn and sad this sacred mound,
    And dear the form which here doth rest!—
O lightly lie, sweet flowery turf,
    Thou veil'st a sainted mother's breast!

A cheering beam has left my path,
    Beneath this stone rests its pale ray;
I ne'er have known a warmer beam,
    Nor can I 'till life's latest day.

Ah! who can feel that time has power
    To break the spell—refill life's bowl,—
When heart from heart by death is torn,
    And rent asunder soul from soul?

Thrice has the hawthorn budded—bloomed,
    Since o'er this grave my heart first bled,—
And these pale flowers I planted then,
    Have thrice their mournful offerings shed.

Yet O whene'er I dream of her,
  That slumbering chord—before so still,—
Awakes, her image to restore,
  And my whole soul with sorrow fill.

This heart, bereft, time cannot heal,
  Nor bring the loved one back to me;
But bear my pilgrim footsteps on,
  To meet her 'yond the silent sea!

THE TRUE FRIEND.

Of all the valued things of earth,
   There's none I value half as high
As one true friend, on whom to lean
   And to implicitly rely.

And I have one, yea, I have more,—
   Yet clouds and shadows tell the best;
When our sun shines, false friends are near,
   But when 'tis clouded—that's the test.

When the sun shines, our shadows come
   And follow very near;
But if a cloud obscures his beams,
   Then quick the shadows disappear.

The true friend has a heart to feel,—
   With you his joys, his griefs divide,—
Nor, like the publican of old,
   Will pass by on the other side.

Friend in adversity, my soul
  Doth closely cleave to thee!
No other one I own as friend,
  Whatever his professions be.

MY FATHER'S BIBLE.

This was my father's blessed book;
   Just ere he died he gave it me;
How precious is the sacred gift,
   This valued legacy!

How soiled and worn is every page!
   On every single leaf I trace
Some mark which to my heart to-day,
   Brings back his reverent face.

On its worn cover is my name;
   Till now I did not know 'twas here;
This tender token of his care
   Makes it still doubly dear.

Writ by the trembling hand of age,
   Which, in my infant day,
He often laid upon my head,
   And taught me how to pray.

The pious counsels he then gave,
   Are lingering with me yet;

AN AUTUMNAL WREATH.

Tho' my right hand its cunning lose,
   These I can ne'er forget.

Associations tender, sweet,
   And thronging memories dear,
Come as I trace each well-worn leaf,
   Again we all are here.

Linger, delightful moments stay!
   I see each dear, familiar face;
Before we speak the last adieu,
   One tender, fond embrace.

I see a mother's sainted face;
   A truer heart I ne'er have known;
Long, long ago, that heart was dust,
   With rank grass overgrown.

And now my heart, like some lone bird
   Brooding upon its nest,
Recalls thy last remembered word,
   O mother! dearest! best!

Here on this consecrated hearth,
   This Mecca of my heart,
Here midst the hallowed joys of home,
   This volume formed a part.

She read its pages o'er and o'er;
　On it I've seen her drop a tear,
While reading of the suffering Christ,
　Who to her soul was dear.

O book of books, divine bequest!
　From thee I never more can part;
Be thou a sacred heirloom kept,
　Loved relic of a father's heart.

MY FATHER'S BURIAL HOUR.

'Tis two o'clock,—ah, solemn hour!
   Thank heaven that I am left alone!
Sacred to sorrow be this day,
   With dark clouds o'er it thrown.

Friends write, "this hour they bury him."
   Our father,—dearest, best:
O can it be that Death's cold hand
   Lies heavy on thy breast?—

That breast where oft we leaned our head,
   In childhood's helpless day,
Is that heart still'd which beat for us,
   Pulseless and cold as clay?

Those hands which toiled till callous grown,
   For those thou loved'st so well,
Say, has the icy hand of death
   Bound with his mystic spell?

Now other feet than thine do move
   To bear thee to thy silent bed,

Where, in the dust, thy loved one long
   Hath lain her weary head.

I seem to hear the frozen clods
   Fall on thy coffin-lid;
O God, forgive me if I grieve
   That they that face have hid.

My soul, O look not in that grave;
   My dear ones are not there;
'Tis only dust that dust can claim,—
   With life it hath no share.

Grave, take this sacred, silent dust,
   So precious to our sorrowing heart!
We know 'tis dust, and only dust,
   But O how loth to part!

To hear no more on earth that voice,
   To see no more that smile,
That smile no more to cheer our hearts,
   Nor voice our grief beguile.

Our God, we feel we're not alone,
   That pained hearts grieve the wide world o'er;
The burdened air is full of sighs,
   Which souls bereft incessant pour.

It must be so until that tree,
   Which yields the fruit of death, shall die;
Until this earth grows dim with age,
   And Time fulfils his destiny.

'Tis done,—earth wraps her winding-sheet
   About the form we love so well;
Our mourners go about the street;
   Thy will be done—O God! 'tis well.

THE DEAREST NAME.

A saint upon his death-bed lay,
    As the sun was going down,
While angels, up in Paradise,
    Were weaving a christian's crown.

And friends came round his dying bed,
    And wept a last farewell;
Faintly he murmured, "Strangers, these,
    Whose names I cannot tell."

His dearest friend he did not know,—
    Familiar names were all forgot;
When fondly pressed to speak loved names,
    He said, "I know them not."

"Do you know Jesus Christ?" said one;
    "Jesus Christ, my dear?"
"Oh, yes! that name, I know it well,
    And have for many a year."

A heavenly smile lit up his face,
    That blest name quivered on his lips;

And, in a moment more, his eyes
   Were closed in death's eclipse.

And when the sun had sunk behind
   The hills along the west,
Another soul, whom Jesus loved,
   Reposed upon his breast.

O Christ! when I shall pass the vale,
   May thy dear name fall on mine ear;
That heavenly, sweet, divinest name,
   Even in death I'd pause to hear.

"JESUS WEPT."

"Jesus wept!" O may not we,
    If tears have moistened eyes Divine?
Jesus, lover of all souls,
    Saviour of the world, thou 'rt mine!

Lamb of God! meek, patient one,
    Thou wert shelterless amidst the blast;
Grief was thy companion here,—
    A man of sorrows to the last.

Whilst thou wast in the world, O Christ!
    Tears oft bedewed thy pensive face;
Weighed down with sorrow for mankind,—
    Thy Father's gift, the human race.

We weep for very grief, our Lord,
    When we recall Gethsemane;
When none could watch one single hour,
    None keep awake to pray with thee.

What wonder, then, that blood-like sweat
    Fell from thy face upon the ground,

When thou alone, pale watcher, prayed,
  In sorrow, deep, profound.

'Tis eve,—I think of that sad night,
  When thou wast shamefully betrayed;
When he of the black heart drew nigh,
  With spear and sword of burnished blade.

Exalted at thy Father's side,
  Thou need'st not our poor sympathy;
Yet, did not tears relieve our heart,
  The very rocks would sigh.

I look up to the silent moon,
  Now coursing onward through the sky;
Full grateful to that pale-faced orb,
  Which watched above thine agony.

And while the night doth weep its tears
  Over a sinful world asleep,
I would commune with thee, dear Lord,—
  Thou who on earth didst often weep.

The travail of thy suffering soul,
  Dear Christ, thine eyes shall see;
A world redeemed from every stain,
  Thine holy heritage shall be.

The dust whereon thy feet have trod,
    In woods and vales, is sacred ground;
And on each mount, by every stream,
    Shall righteousness abound.

HOUR OF COMMUNION.

Call me not down, ye carking cares,
    I worship to-night in my closet high;
Wearily toiling through the day,
    As the sun goes down, " I say good bye."

Good bye to suffering, pain, and grief,
    To every care I say good bye;
By the joy of one hour alone with God,
    I charge ye that ye come not nigh.

Dear Lord, I hither come to pray,
    And to confess all wrong I've done;
My sorrows all I tell to thee,
    Most merciful and Holy One!

If in my heart one sin has found
    To-day a welcome lurking place,
O pluck it thence, and be it cast
    Into the depths of pardoning grace.

If there's a cup which I must drink,
    Which maketh life a weariness,

I would not pray to have it pass,
   But drink up all its bitterness.

If evermore my feet must press
   The furnace floor I long have trod,
O be his presence near to bless,
   Whose form was like the Son of God.

MY ALL — MY ALL.

A holy, sweet, remembered hour
   There was, which I can ne'er forget;
Its glory shines around me still,
   And all its sweetness lingers yet:
A balm to heal in sore distress,
A light to cheer my gloominess.

Like an oasis midst the sand,
   A cool, green spot on which I rest,
Oft as its memory returns,
   O how supremely I am blessed:
For with the memory of that hour,
Returns its consecrating powers.

A solitary suffering one,
   No eye but heaven's my gloom did see,
None knew the gloomy days and weeks
   Which were consuming me;
Unless some pitying angels' gaze,
Was watching o'er those troubled days.

A haunting gloom had round me lain;
　Where e'er I went the ghost pursued,
Like the dark shades of destiny,
　Which every morning seemed renewed;
Darker grew each returning day,
Till hope, at last, had fled away.

A dread of something undefined,
　A shrinking from some hidden ill,
It was not madness, it was not grief,
　'Twas something sorer still,—
A nameless something, undefined,
Which held in thrall my tortured mind.

No guilt upon my soul did lie,
　No concious wrong my heart oppressed;
Yet, like a black, cold, leaden shroud,
　A dead weight lay upon my breast;
And darker life each moment grew,
Till not a gleam of light shone through.

Night seemed not darker than the morn,
　For everywhere was sick'ning gloom;
My idols all had turned to clay,
　My flowers all lost their sweetest bloom;
Their roots seemed twining round a bier,
And on each leaf trembled a tear.

In tearless agony, cried I,
  Dear Lord I at thy feet would fall:
There is no helper, none but thee,
  Thou art my all, my all!
Then pitying eyes above me bent
And lo! the Comforter was sent.

A bright, felt presence hovered near,
  And smote the darkness, as of old,
And O that glimpse of glory rare
  He to my spirit did unfold;
'Twas like the Patriarch's ladder, given,
On which my heart ascends to heaven.

For days and days, whene'er I breathed,
  " Thou art my all," in cloistered rest,
The Father 'd draw me to his heart,
  And lay my head upon his breast;
O that blest hour I'll ne'er forget,
Its glory gilds my pathway yet.

Should I forget each tender friend,
  Each pleasant path my feet have trod,
Yet nevermore would I forget
  That sacred hour alone with God;
My all in life, whom I adore;
Nor can I ask or wish for more.

My heart with greatful love o'erflows,
Like Jordan midst the harvest rain:
Prayer, the deep burden of its theme,
And praise the sweet refrain;
Naught but the sinner's sigh I give,
Because *Christ lives*, I too shall live.

TRUST IN GOD.

"Tho' thou slay me, yet will I trust in thee."

As the sick child doth lay its heart
   Upon its mother's own,
So, trustful, I would lay my cares,
   O Father, 'neath thy throne.

And I would lay my human heart,
   An offering, all unmeet,
A hopeful, trembling, humble thing,
   Beneath thy mercy-seat.

In penitence I bow me down
   And lay my head low in the dust,
Whisper a prayer, and breathe the words,
   "Altho' thou slay me, yet I'll trust."

I'd freight my humble bark with prayer,
   And send it forth with faith and trust;
Tho' often hid beneath the waves,
   Yet trust in thee, Father, I must,

THE GOOD OLD PILGRIM.

One day, it was long time ago,
    A weary pilgrim came our way;
He turned in here, that holy man,
    And we urged him hard to stay.

And here he gladly stayed with us,
    To rest, to sing, and pray;
And our hearts did burn with love to him,
    That old disciple gray.

He was one of heaven's anointed ones,
    Gray-bearded, lowly, bent with age;
Elisha-like, the man of God,
    The healer, prophet, sage.

He had sown broad fields where others reap'd,
    The seed of truth had scattered wide;
A stranger pilgrim in the world,
    Proclaiming Christ the crucified.

At length the pilgrim bent his steps
    Toward the southern cross to die;

And Israel's chariots met him there,
    And bore him to his home on high.

Now, like a ripened shock of corn,
    The saint is gathered in,—
Into the holy garner, where
    There's no more death nor sin.

Now where the orange-tree doth bloom
    'Neath Carolina's sod,
Watched by filial love and care,
    Doth rest the man of God.

O mantle of the pilgrim, rest
    On us, who've waited long,
And in the pilgrim's chamber poured
    Unheard our plaintive song.

INTEMPERANCE.

I have not seen the sanguine field
    Where stalks the war-god o'er the plain,
Where dark-browed vengeance thirsts for blood,
    And feasts the vulture on the slain,
Nor seen the death-shafts flying, when
Were thinn'd the ranks of living men.

Nor have I felt the syrock's breath,
    Which from the arid desert blows,
Scattering the red-hot sand of death
    As o'er the burning plain it goes.
I know a fire more sure to kill,
Which smoulders in the burning still.

I have not seen the plague-spot drear,
    Piling in heaps the unsightly dead,
Nor heard the pale horse tramping near
    With awful, solemn tread;
Yet seen a plague-spot direr far
Than syrock's breath, or murderous war.

Grim slavery has been strangled—dead;
   Yet in our country doth remain
A form which stalks with direr tread,
   All o'er our fair domain.
A venomed reptile—sure to kill,—
It is the deathworm of the still.

The grain which should the hungry feed,
   Fattens that reptile of the still;
And hard, laborious hands do toil
   For poison which doth slowly kill.
O that dread evil, deadlier far
Than slavery or devasting war.

Woe, woe to you, ye men of blood!
   Ye who do smite the orphaned-head,
Who fill your coffers with the gold
   Which should have bought them bread;
O know you not the bowls you fill
Will breed for you a viper-ill
Which will eat into your hard heart's core,
And rankle there forevermore?

O ye, who worketh night and day
   To swell the score of joyless homes,
Where hunger gaunt finds its abode
   And squalid misery comes,
You're gold is cankered with a rust
Which kills your hearts—you are accurs'd.

Bow not at that vile monarch's shrine,
Who praised the gods and drank the wine,
While he, presiding at the feast,
Was but a gorgeous, kingly beast,
And you his destiny may share,—
O selfish ones, beware, beware!

Ye who our country's laws do make,
  Beseechingly we look to you;
We plead with you, for conscience's sake,
  This one good act of justice do:
Strike at the evil's fountain-head,
  Turn not our sheaves into a curse,
Let not the swelling ears of grain
  A damning evil nurse.

Enact some fearful penalty,
  For all who do the poison bring;
And let no ship from o'er the main
  Discharge the deadly thing.

TO PIUS IX.

Scourge of the world! relentless one!
    Puffed up with superstitious pride,—
Thy hands are stained with martyrs blood,
    Who have for truth and conscience died!

From thy red throne thou dost look down
    On cringing minions, who do hate
The purple of thy tottering throne,
    And thy mock majesty of state.

That proud bird's plumes which o'er thee nod,
    They feel are thine and their disgrace;
And while they cringe and bend the knee,
    They inly curse thee to thy face.

Grim darkening power, thou turn'st the key
    Of knowledge on thy human kind,
And seat'st thyself in God's own place,
    Thou blindest leader of the blind.

And so thou art infallible?—
    Would have thy priests declare thee so?—

Sure *God* doth *not* regard thee thus,—
   Know this, poor weakling, know.

Dress up thy dolls, weak, pampered thing,
   And set them on each highway fence,
To wring from bony, breadless hands,
   The meagre, hard-earned Peter-pence.

The scarlet hat, the childish toys,
   The relic skulls, the bells and beads,—
Go, offer them a sacrifice,
   For thy poor starvelings needs,

Whose sunken eyes, and trembling limbs
   Attest the hunger long endured!
Unbar the cold, dark dungeon, where
   Thy victims long have been immured.

Send forth thy hirelings o'er the sea,
   Where liberty was born and nursed,
Where despots, fouled with blood like thee,
   Will evermore be cursed.

The eagle of the western world
   May yet on thy foul cage descend,
When 'tis too late for thee to learn,
   His might to conquer and defend.

Vain dost thou seek to gather strength
   From this *vast, free domain;*
Thy refugees, thick gathered here,
   Reap their broad fields of grain.

There no bare-footed, hungry monks,—
   Scarce aught but skin and bones,—
Do crouch and beg the children's bread,
   In sniveling, pious tones.

Isle of Caprera, thou dost hold one patriot heart,
   And patriot swords are waiting there,
The blood upon their burnished edge
   Ere long may crimson berries bear.

Venice, fair daughter of that sea
   Whose waters oft have reddened deep,
A pure form walks thy streets to-day,
   Which nevermore will sleep.

Jealous for freedom's holy cause,
   She oft has spurned the iron heel;
Beware, thou foe to liberty,
   E'en now thy throne doth reel!

Italia now in sackcloth mourns,
   While baffled patriots often meet
To curse the weakling on his throne,
   Who kneels to kiss a coward's feet.

While he, that dastard thing of France,
    Led on by silken apron-strings,
Doth take the crosier and the crown,
    And flaunt them in the face of kings.

Had'st thou the power of other days,
    When a crowned head, degraded low,
Compell'd by dark despotic power,
    Did kiss a vile, detested toe.

The inquisition, rack, and stake,
    Would run with blood, as they did of old,
Ere light broke through Rome's massive walls,
    And loosed thy fiendish hold.

Let folly drop the unholy mask,
    No longer play the tyrant-fool,
No more degrade the christian name,
    Nor make Christ's hallowed cross thy tool.

The gold and ermine of thy robes
    Of scarlet, in the dust will lie,
When thou wilt look in vain for help,
    With sad, despairing eye.

Remorse, the vulture in thine heart,
    Will someday plunge his bloody beak,
When thou, the victim of thy sins,
    In vain for help will seek.

No holy (?) unction then can heal
　　The sore which long must fester there:
No smoke of gums, from censers borne,
　　Can move the Virgin's prayer.

God's prophet has foretold thine end,—
　　Tho' long it linger, it must come,
Thou and thy throne must surely fall
　　To make for truth and justice room.

THE PRESENT EPOCH.

Era of great achievements,
   Of high, immortal deeds;
When men begin to see and feel
   Humanity's great needs.

The time for casting down of thrones
   Has fully come at last;
The surging of the sea, the winds,
   Echo the bugle's blast.

The watchers on heaven's ramparts cry:—
   "The harvest time is near,—
Gird on thy sword of truth, O man!
   Awake, thou slumbering seer!"

The fields are whitening in the sun,
   And soon the olive tree will bloom;
Error is writhing in its coils,
   In dread of certain doom.

Better by far the martyr's death
   Than ignorance and inglorious ease;
We now the bloody tokens hail,
   As signs of universal peace.

All nations are aroused at last,—
  Deep calleth unto deep,—
The embryo giant, Liberty,
  In darkness can no longer sleep.

Strict justice, right, equality,
  Man's birthright, heaven's eternal boon,
Are marching on with rapid strides,
  And nearing their high noon.

Break time, worn fetters of the past;
  Perish each creed that's formed to bind
The heavy burdens on the weak,
  Which darken the immortal mind.

That horse-leech power which crieth give,—
  Give for thy soul's eternal life,—
Which stalks arrayed in ill-got gold,
  Scattering the seeds of strife,—

Which crieth until it is hoarse,
  For all the world to come;
To come well mailed, in steel and brass,
  With banners, sword, and drum,—

To come with crosier and with cross,
  With carnal weapons, dyed in blood;
Cries come! defend my holiness (?)
  Ye faithful, true, and good.

The west doth hear that thirsty cry
   Which thirsts for power and gold;
The east, aroused, cries to the west
   Its destinies to mould.

Action, bold action, is the power
   Which doth take hold on circumstance;
No folding now of nerveless hands,
   If freedom's cause we would advance.

GARIBALDI.

Incarnate liberty!
    Brave son of freedom's sire!
Tho' scarred by the battle-axe of war,
    Still glows thy patriot fire!

Loved as a brother! I have watched thy ways
    As I have marked some kindly beaming star;
Rejoicing in thy triumph, just and right,
    Borne to my ear from far.

Let thy young eagles rest awhile,
    And fledge their wings of might,
While the dismal groans from the vatican
    Suggests another's flight.

Brave pioneer of liberty!
    Thine annals brightly shine,
Like a star of the first magnitude
    Along Italia's line.

Vainly they strive to shut thee in
    On thy green ocean-isle;

And vain the Swiss would seek to hold
    Mazzinna still the while.

Now foul-mouthed blood-hounds
    Haunt the steps of righteous liberty;
But yet, with all their hidden craft,
    Can ne'er arrest its destiny.

The world has had its heroes,
    Martyrs for liberty,
But none have yet more nobly fought
    For wronged humanity.

The spirit of the noble sire
    Goes with the patriot son
To consummate the righteous work
    The father has begun.

O hater of the scarlet breast!
    Whose spies are on thy track,
Whose thunders and anathemas
    Have failed to bring thee back.

That evil genius! that grim cloud
    Which thrusts itself 'twixt God and man,
Which seeks with its deceiving wiles
    The universe to span.

Watch thou, with piercing, eagle eye,—
  Now with Mazzinna seize thy chance,
And on Rome's hated den of wrong,
  With steady steps advance.

Infallibility may fall
  Before thy valiant sword;
For righteous judgment shall prevail,—
  Thus saith the righteous Lord.

Liberty triumphs everywhere;
  But within Rome's hated walls,
Where crime which hides its head by day,
  The darkened night appals.

Zealous for righteousness and truth,
  Impatiently we wait:
We stretch our hands, and fervent pray,
  Like Bartimeus at mercy's gate.

IMPROMPTU.

The more I learn
   Of governments and men,
The more I know of what is,
   And what has been,
      Closer, dear Lord,
My heart clings unto thee,
For I in *all* thy love and wisdom see!
Kingdoms and men
   Alike are born to prove
That God's eternal
   Changeless law, is love.

THE LAST DECADE.

Lo! what hath God wrought?
   Be satisfied, O righteous soul!
'Tis that for which thou long hast prayed,
   Which human power cannot control.

Eventful time when slavery fell,
   No more is heard its clanking chains;
We've heard its last expiring groan,
   No vestige of the scourge remains.

We've seen the falling of a throne,
   An impious monarch in the dust;
A tyranny we've seen cast down,
   Which long the world hath curs'd.

Babylon is falling now,
   Her scarlet robes trail in the dust:
Lo,—the beginning of the end,
   No more in chariots can she trust.

Those who have shed the blood of saints,
   Now drinketh blood for blood;

Righteous art thou, O Lord of Hosts!
And all thy ways are good.

Lo, the fifth angel pours his wrath
Upon the foul den of the beast;
He gnaws his tongue for very pain,
And hungry vultures throng the feast.

THE PLACE OF JUDGMENT.

"Behold the righteous shall be recompensed in the earth; much more the wicked and the sinner."— *Prov.* 11:31.

"Verily he is a God that judgeth in the earth."— *Psalms*, 58:11.

"And Jesus said, for judgment am I come into this world."— *John*, 9:39.

Tradition saith, that on a time
   A holy man was called to ascend
To Sinai's consecrated height,
   Where, lo! Jehovah did attend.

Awed by the glory of the sight,
   Moses fell at the feet of Him
Who, veiled in dazzling brightness stood,
   Between the cherubim.

He spake, "My son, arise, give ear,
   I'll show thee strange, mysterious scenes;
Knowledge too wonderful for thee,
   Yet I will tell thee what it means."

Beloved, I order all events,
   However great they seem, or small;

I Am! — I cradled thee upon the Nile,
    And my watchful care is over *all*.

Love prompted me to form a world,—
    To bless and people every part;
And every creature whom I've made
    I bear upon my heart.

In love, not anger, I correct,—
    Thus disciplining every one;
My council evermore will stand,
    And all my will be done.

My government is one vast chain
    Linked with each human soul;
And not the slightest jar is made
    But agitates the whole.

No finite power can make or mar,
    No cunning frustrate my design;
To accomplish all I have proposed,—
    Can disappointment e'er be mine?

I write my law on every heart,
    I give a conscience quick to test,
Yet do no violence to the will,
    For each one does as seems him best.

Man blindly works my righteous will,
　And naught can ever mar my plan;
Co-workers, they my schemes advance,
　Which are to form the perfect man.

Each his appointed lot accepts,—
　Each walks the path I've marked for him;
His bounds are set, nor can he pass
　The shadow of the dial, dim.

The number of his days were fixed,
　Or ever time with him begun;
He must live his allotted time,
　Till the last sand of life has run.

My attributes all harmonize,
　Combine, and show a perfect whole;
I of one blood have made mankind,
　And yearn with love for every soul.

A love more warm and tender far,
　Than any mother bears her child;
She may forget,—she may forsake,—
　As doth the desert-ostrich wild.

Yet nevermore can I forget,—
　They're graven on my heart and palms;
No power can hinder my design
　To draw my offspring to my arms.

Men call evil, good; good, evil call;
   A mystery not understood;
Yet know that I have ordered all,
   And work to consummate the good.

Absolute evil, there is none;
   Good, oft the garb of evil wears;
And tho' *man* may not this discern,
   To *me all good* appears.

Would I create a power to war
   Against myself, the Infinite?—
Let finite weakness rule the world,
   And darkness shroud the eternal light?

Would justice my high attribute
   Which poises the impartial scale,
Create an image of myself,
   Knowing its endless bliss would fail?

If I were partial in my love,
   And cared for only a small part,
Say, who could draw the awful line
   'Twixt these and those most near my heart?

In knowledge I am infinite,
   Each circumstance part of my plan;
And each event and circumstance
   Progresses and develops man.

Thus out of evil good doth come,
    And out of sorrow joy doth spring;
Absolute evil would be vain,—
    A noisome, useless thing.

Think you I work without design?
    That I created all your race
Without a single thought or care,
    But left each one to find his place?

But as I work with an intent,
    It ever must be wise and good;
Since in my essence I am love,—
    How else can it be understood?

Thwarted I have never been,
    Nor disappointed can I be;
All things in heaven and earth combine
    To work out man's high destiny.

I overturn, and overturn,
    And purify the gold from dross;
And so far down the lapse of time,
    My Christ will die upon the cross.*

*Acts 3: 18.

A Peter will deny his name,
  A Judas will his blood betray,
This is my council, this my plan,*
  And down the years I've fixed the day.†

What to mankind is not now known,
  Hereafter they shall know;
And in all things which I have done
  They will rejoicing bow.

My judgments all are in the earth,
  And here I punish every sin;
Here Christ will reign in righteousness
  'Till all souls are brought in.

Unscathed, unspotted, undefiled,
  The soul returns to me once more,
As sinless as when first it burned
  Upon the verge of earth's dim shore.

No sin can soil the deathless part,—
  Forever pure it must remain;
Tho' agonizing oft while here,
  'Twill be set free without a stain.

And with one shepherd in one fold,
  All the highest bliss shall find,

*Acts 2: 23.   †Acts 4: 27, 28.

In raveling out the warp and woof,
   And plan of the Infinite Mind.

In Persia and in Babylon,
   My people captive long were kept;
On willows hung their silent harps,
   And by the mournful river wept.

Far from the country of their birth
   They learned to desecrate my name;
To bow them down to stocks and stones,
   And pass to Moloch through the flame.

As the thirsty kine the water drink,
   So errors they drank in;
Devoutly bowed to stocks and stones,
   And taught the unweaned child to sin.

They, by this sad experience, learned
   The falseness of the heathen lore;
And in deep, humble penitence,
   Returned to me once more.

Thus all things ever work for good,
   I *order naught in vain;*
Neither the drouth which smites the earth,
   Nor the overflowing rain.

I will illustrate now, my son,
  How from seeming evil cometh good;
And now present to you a scene
  By which it may be understood.

Turn now thine eyes towards the south,
  Where glitters Ophir's golden ore,
And tell me what thou dost behold,
  Then I will show thee more.

How men work out their destiny,—
  How I fulfil my every plan;
How I make all events combine
  To bless and perfect man.

Be not dismayed; look down the mine,
  And, till the scene is done,
Mark well what passes in thy sight,—
  What seest thou, now, my son?

I see two men who delve for gold
  In the deep, glittering mine,—
Yes, I have lain that gold away,
  To further my design.

What else?—One with deadly blow
  Fells the other to the ground;

You shudder at this cruel deed,
   To you a mystery profound.

One is Avarice—not content
   With all his golden store,
He steals the other's hard-earned wealth,
   Then strikes him to the floor.

He hides the treasure 'neath a stone,
   Then hurries swift away;
But he must pay the penalty
   In another day.

What more?—I see a soldier pass that way,—
   He stumbles on the hidden gold:
He clutches it with eager hand,
   And hurries from the wold.

What else?—I see that soldier on a beast,
   Hump-backed and small-eared;
He rides with swift and silent speed,
   As if pursuit he feared.

With slackened speed he nears a spring,—
   His camel kneels for him to drink;
When, lo! he drops a bag of gold,
   Close by the cooling brink.

Unconcious of his loss, he rides
   And speeds away from view,—
What more dost see that's dark and strange?
   Dost thou see aught that's new?

A lad comes skipping down the way,
   Whistling with boyish glee;
He sees and grasps the bag of gold,
   And speedily doth flee.

What more? A poor old man bent low with age,
   Comes tottering to the brink,
And seats him on a mossy stone
   Where the soldier stopp'd to drink.

What else? I see the soldier speeding back,
   In search of his lost store;
He now confronts the poor old man,
   Searching him o'er and o'er.

He strikes him dead upon the spot,—
   O 'tis a mystery indeed!
That he, the old grey-headed man,
   Thus cruelly should bleed.

Oppress'd with guilt, grown gray with age,
   He comes with tottering step and failing eyes;
The blood which long ago he shed,
   Loudly for justice cries.

Now justice does assert its right,—
  The father of the lad he killed,
While working in rich Ophir's mines,
  And the soldier now his blood has spilled.

The gold is where it does belong;
  Each one has done as seemed him best:
I've done no violence to their will,
  Yet justice has its high behest.

The lad a holy man becomes,—
  Makes my name known in other lands,—
Scatters the gold to bless the poor,
  With generous, liberal hands.

Man cannot fathom my designs,—
  The problem dark of good and ill;
There's a limit to the human mind,
  But all do blindly work my will.

Now, my son, thou may'st depart,
  And from this holy mount descend:—
I'll order all thy ways aright,
  And I will guide thee to the end,

Till thou shalt stand on Nebo's height,
  To thence go down no more;
There, thou may'st view the promised land,
  But thou must not go o'er.

And there my angel will descend,
    And receive thy parting soul,
And thou shalt with thy fathers live,
    While heaven's vast ages roll,

Where they needeth not the sun by day,
    Neither the moon by night;
For I shall ever walk therein,
    And be their life, their light.

Tears from all faces will be wiped,—
    No pain can ever enter there;
No poisonous breath can ever come,
    To taint the balmy air.

Thy form I'll hide in Moab's vale,
    Where 'twill return to dust; *
But thy spirit shall return to me,
    From whence it came at first.

---

* Then shall the dust return to the earth as it was, and the spirit shall return unto God, who gave it.—*Eccl.* 12:7.

THE WINGED HOURS.

The hours, the winged hours,
    Born of bright moments which have fled;
With lightning speed, they fly away
    To join their ghosts among the dead.
The record of the past is borne
From whence no traveller doth return

The winged hours, the natal hour,
    Dawns on a feeble spark of life:
It from the source of being comes
    To mingle in the mortal strife;
A spark, enkindled, which shall burn
When worlds on worlds to dust return.

The hours, the fleeting sunny hours,
    When hope and love inspires the breast,
Their radiance o'er our pathway thrown,
    With beauty every scene invests.
Linger, sweet hours, forever stay,
Haste not on thy bright wings away.

The hour, the hour, the bridal hour,
    How fraught with anxious hopes and fears;
How gayly chime the marriage-bells
    'Midst smiles of joy and silent tears;
The mystic union,—heart to heart,
Together joined till death shall part.

The hour, the hour, the winged hour,
    Which ushers in the infant year,
With snow-white tablet on its breast
    As yet unsullied with a tear.
Crimes may stand there a dark array,
No angel's tears can wash away.

The hour, departing, solemn hour,
    Which bears the dying year away;
Year follows year, how quick they glide
    Adown the gulf of time's dark tide,
Receding swiftly from our view,—
Pale, dying year, farewell, adieu.

The hours, the hours, the winged hours,
    Soon we no more on earth will roam;
Nightly we pitch our time-worn tent,
    "A day's march nearer home."
Poor, frail ephemeras of a day,
Like a shepherd's tent, we pass away.

The hour, the hour, the dying hour,
  O hour of all life's hours the best!
When the tried spirit plumes its wings,
  And soars to everlasting rest;
No more to sorrow, grieve, or sigh,
No more to languish, pine, or die.

HE IS NOT HERE.

I've walked all day among the flowers,
   Listening to a sad undertone:
He is not here, doth seem to come
   On every breeze that's borne;
To every sound, distant or near,
   Echo repeats, "He is not here."

The sun pours out his golden light,
   Shining with his divinest rays,
Yet there is such a lonesome gloom,—
   It is the gloomiest of all days;
Written with sunbeams, far and near,
I read and feel, "He is not here."

The air bends down with fragrance
   Breathed from the heart of flowers,
And my favorite bird doth sing
   In the greenest of all bowers:
She seems to feel that he's away,
And sings, "He will not come to-day."

The purple fruit hangs clustering
   Upon the pendant vine,

Waiting the husbandman's return
  To press the generous wine;
O love, which woke in Paradise,
Thou still dost live 'neath northern skies!

My heart has fears I may not own,
  Which others know not of;
Why was I made to suffer pangs
  At which some friends but scoff!
O suffering, so sore, intense,
Will joy not sometime recompense?

I fear disease has lain him low,
  Afar from me and home;
Why hastens not some carrier-dove
  To summons me to come?
O kind, electric wire, just say
That he still lives, tho' far away!

O treacherous sea! hast thou engulfed
  His form with other forms,
Which lie far down in ocean caves,
  The sport of wind and storms?
Thou can'st not keep his heart, O sea!
For it belongs to God and me.

The days seem lengthened into months,
  The hours like days appear,

The lagging sun seems not to move,
    As if a Joshua held him here;
And yet, O sun, I'd have thee stay,
Nor set while he is far away.

The sun is down, and here I sit,
    And sadly ponder o'er
The lone, prospective hours to come
    Should he return no more;
What would life be bereft of one
My heart so long has leaned upon?

Night and the darkness deepen fast,
    While silently I pensive gaze
Upon yon mournful evening star,
    And think of happier days,
When thou wast here, O friend of mine,
With my hand fondly clasped in thine.

O for some sympathizing soul
    Whereon to lean my trembling heart:
One who can so intensely feel,
    As of my fears to share some part,—
One feeling soul to bear with me
My deep suspense and agony.

What do I hear?— The rumbling cars;
    But now my heart is beating so

I cannot tell from whence they come,
   Whether they halt, or onward go;
They've gone afar, but still I hear,
While the sound dies, "He is not here."

'Tis midnight,—I have waited long;
   Again the iron horse does come;
O heaven! that this last train might bear
   The loved one to his home.
A voice which fills me with affright
Says, "Dead! he will not come to-night."

Rumbling along the dark, deep track,
   Each signal seems a solemn wail,
The night — how dark and sad it seems,
   My very heart doth fail;
Absence and death seem twin-born here,
"He is not here," O no, nor near.

The last train gone, all silent now,
   Save the watch-dog's mournful bark;
Darkness and silence reign supreme,
   Again I listen — *hark!*
Can it be his, that step I hear?
How my heart throbs with hope and fear!

A well-known step comes up the path,
   A hand familiar lifts the latch,

Within the hall my eager ear
    A loving voice doth catch,
I listen now with 'bated breath,
As if hung on it life or death.

Somehow the firelight on the wall
    A sort of tender glory seems,—
Just like the light I've sometimes seen
    In sweet, remembered dreams;
Dreams which I'd never have depart,
But stay forever with my heart.

COMPENSATION.

For every pang we feel
   A joy is given,
And sorrow soon doth end
   In the heart that's riven.

Every hot tear we shed
   Is bottled up,
And for each bitter grief
   A balm is in our cup,

And sometimes when we mourn
   The loved and lost,
The vacant chair is filled
   By one we love the most.

For every stormy day
   Sunshine doth come,
And for every homeless one
   Each place is home.

Where the field is deepest burned
   Greenest the grass doth spring,

And where the lightning rent the oak,
  Birds build and sing.

Where the Nile o'erflows its banks,
  Laying cot and palace low,
It compensation brings,
  For more rank the corn will grow.

When sounds the bugle blast,
  Trembling with war's alarm,
It prophesyeth good
  Far more than harm.

For ne'er a war began
  But God did hold the sword,
And none did ever cease
  But at his word.

Gladly we'll take the cup
  Prepared by one who knows
How to protect the right
  Amidst its foes.

THE AUTUMN OF LIFE.

Loved one, gather up thy mantle,
    Draw its folds around thee close;
For the frost of life is gathering,
    Paling on thy cheek the rose.
Sad yet lovely in its fading,
    Token of a brighter day,
Where immortal life pervading,
    Ends the reign of sad decay;
Usher of the morn eternal,
    Nevermore to pass away.

Years and months and weeks are waning,
    Shorter each succeeding day,
Every beating pulse complaining
    Of the roughness of the way.
No; O no, no! not complaining
    Of the roughness of the way;
But instinctively recoiling
    From the inroads of decay,
And a yearning for the loved ones
    Who have passed away, away.

Well, these hoar-frosts and these short days,
    And this fading of life's flowers,
And the yearning for the loved ones,
    And this failing of life's powers,
Are the means heaven has appointed
    To wean our spirits from the dust;
Even he, God's own anointed,
    Poured the prayer of faith and trust,
For that life which has no ending
    In those climes where live the just.

Then, loved one, gather up thy mantle,
    Shake the dust from off thy feet;
Look beyond the blue remoteness,
    Where congenial spirits meet.

OCTOBER OF LIFE.

My life's October draweth near;
    Heart, gather up what thou hast sown;
And as thou reapest it to-day,
    Thou must the fruitage own.

Autumn's pale finger turns the leaves,
    And writes sage lessons every day;
The fading, withering of the flowers,
    Are all prophetic of decay.

Did I go forth in life's spring-time,
    Weeping, and bearing precious seeds?
If so, my garner's full of grain,
    Without the noxious weeds.

Humbled in dust, I freely own
    My sheaves are few and small;
But as they are I'd offer them,
    Father, to thee,—all—all.

I'd offer them with brimful heart,
    And soul ascending higher;

Father, accept the offering now,
    And answer as by fire.

Thou who art love and truth combined,
    Father of all, and mine;
Thy love to our humanity
    Exceeds the joy of harvest-time.

In youth's bright, sunny, dewy morn,
    Ere we life's uplands gain,
We quaff the mingled cup of life,
    Its pleasures and its pain.

Yet both alike are from thine hand;
    Both blessings in disguise;
Each is a link of the vast chain
    Descending from the skies.

I dare not charge thee, Holy One,
    Whose love doth never fail,
With wrath, and hate, and hot revenge,
    Before which heaven would pale.

Doth the trumpet give a doubtful sound?
    Do watchmen of the night
Fail to perceive the dawn
    Of heaven's divinest light?

Sin yields its bitter fruit,
  Its Sodom apples of unrest;
Yet waits not for the doom of death
  To make us more unblest.

Our primal source is Love;
  And our souls, by instinct, rise
To grasp the pillars of that love
  Which lifts us to the skies.

Then go to thy rest, my soul;
  Heart, go to the grave unfearing;
All the spectres which haunt the vale
  Will vanish in its beaming.

HUSBAND.

Husband — the name that's dearer far
   Than any earthly name to me;
Partner, companion, better-half,
   Are all comprised in thee.

Companion of my daily life,
   Co-partner of my every care,
My better-half in thee I find
   Excellence most rare.

If I call thee by some modern name,
   This dearer name I miss;
Of all the dearest ties of earth,
   There's none more dear than this.

Tho' time and care have thinn'd thy locks,
   And sickness paled thy brow,
Far more than when in manhood's prime,
   Husband, I love thee now.

Thine acts of tenderness and love,
   I hoard in sweetest memory;

The thought of all thy kindness is
    As dear as life to me.

Walking the rough and weary ways
    Along our life's decline,
More firm my failing feet will stand,
    If my hand is clasped in thine.

When stranger feet shall press these floors
    Which ours so long have press'd,
Our feet will rest in yon green tent,
    Where kindred hearts now rest.

Would that the sun of both our lives
    Together might go down,
And at the blessed, pearly gate,
    Together take our crown.

Forgive, dear God, the selfish wish,—
    Humbly I bow at thy behest;
Appointed is the way and time,
    To bring us to our final rest.

BIRTHDAY REFLECTIONS.

Rest, aged heart! thou'rt nearing home,
    And nature claims her due repose;
Far on thy journey thou hast come,
    Since thy life's morning sun arose.

Companionless thou hast not come,
    For with thy being's twilight dawn,
Hope clasped thee to her own strong heart,
    And hand in hand we've journeyed on.

Together culled life's morning flowers,
    And sported on its dewy lawn,
Rested awhile in childhood's bowers,
    But childhood soon was gone.

Tho' life's gay Spring and Summer's gone,
    And Autumn hast'ning to depart,
Tho' sometimes weary, yet not lone,
    For Hope still hugs us to her heart.

'Twas in a year of long ago
    We stood on life's meridian line,

Tho' on our head it left its snow,
   Yet bright our evening star doth shine.

Should age look back with fond regret
   To linger on the lap of Spring?
And should she nevermore forget
   The bird's and nests the Summers bring?

No, we joy that Time has brought us here,
   For brighter grows the onward track,
As swifter speeds each flying year,—
   Nor would we call one moment back.

As well might flowers mourn their decay,
   And grieve to mingle with the dust,
As we, that we must pass away,—
   Heaven so designed at first.

For who would turn the fallow soil,
   And sow the grain in Spring,
But for the rich reward of toil,
   The sheaves the harvest-time doth bring?

'Tis our life's Indian Summer time,
   And earth and sea most tranquil lies;
Autumn, tho' past her early prime,
   Puts on her robes of brilliant dyes.

Soon she will change to solemn gray,
   And her dead leaves will rustle round;
Shorter will grow each chilly day,
   The heralds of a rest profound.

How vain to seek for wealth or fame,—
   We would not chase such phantoms now,
Nor would we wear fame's brightest wreath
   Upon our withered brow.

All that we need, and little more,
   The Father unto us has given;
Grateful we count our mercies o'er,
   And offer praise to heaven.

Tho' we of grief have borne our part,
   Yet sheaves of joy we've often reaped;
And full to bursting is our heart,
   Of garnered memories sacred kept.

Shall we not bear them to yon height,
   Where Love shall glow with holier fire,—
Where Faith shall be transformed to sight,
   And in fruition Hope expire?

We do not dread the dire demand
   Which calls the spirit from its clay;

The key is in our Father's hand,
  And the dear Christ has led the way.

Yet we've a mission to fulfil
  Before our destined course is run;
With heart, and hand, and earnest will,
  We'd work until our day is done.

Then let life's Winter come and drop
  Its dead leaves on our clay-walled home,
They are but heralds of a hope,
  Bright garlands for our rest, the tomb.

IN SICKNESS.

Long pale disease has on me preyed,
    With all its train of saddening ills,
Till the spirit, weary of its clay,
    Would fly to the eternal hills.

This constant loosening of the springs,
    Weakening the citadel of life,—
Sometimes I long for the last blow
    To end the painful strife.

Earth, thou hast not one thornless rose;
    Not one unmingled cup of bliss!
Why turn, O heart! from yon bright world,
    And fondly cling to this?—

Where suffering darkens every scene,
    Where no sweet bird sings o'er its nest,
Where, like a train of mourners, pass
    The ghosts of healthful days so blest.

Wert thou not near, O blessed Hope!
    Wert thou a stranger to my breast;
Through all these weary days of pain,
    I should be so unblest.

O Hope! bright candle of the Lord,
   Still light my weary way;
Be thou a lamp my feet to guide
   Unto the perfect day.

LINES ON THE DEATH OF ALICE CARY.

Ah, me! is the sweet singer gone?
    We scarcely felt that she could die;
So thick hopes cluster round the good,
    We almost challenge destiny.

One whom, not having seen, we loved
    With a tender, christian grace;
And on our heart is deep engraved
    Her sainted form and face.

We loved to hear her varied notes,
    The western hills among;
Were glad to fold our feeble wings
    And listen when she sung.

We learned to love her for the love
    She bore for the oppressed;
And the sweet charity which taught
    That all in Christ are blest.

When the seraphic convoy came,
    To guide the spirit's heavenward flight,

Were not the clouds she sometimes feared
   Ablaze with glorious light?

What were the beatific sights
   When ceased the laboring breath,
And the enfranchised spirit learned
   The mystery of Death?

While grief sat robed in sackcloth here,
   Yet not in sad despair;
All hail! from pentecostal lips,
   Greeted her entrance there.

Alas! her harp is silent here,—
   Another minstrel's gone to rest!
But a new-strung lyre awakes above,
   And a sweet saint's among the blest.

But sad that home, so darkened now,
   Where all was light and love refined;
Most sore bereft a sister heart,
   Where tender memories are enshrined.

Could we but comfort that lone heart
   With our poor, stranger sympathy,
The sacred duty should be ours,
   Yet fear 'twould seem but mockery.

Had we the power to draw the veil,
    Or lift the everlasting door,—
Could we but see her as she was,
    The same,—now infinitely more,—

The marks of suffering all erased,
    Exalted, all immortal now,
The late pale face, aglow with health,
    With heaven's own radiance on her brow,—

With all the love she here possess'd,
    And all which heaven doth now bestow,—
With tender pity in her eyes,
    Gazing on her friends below.

O sister of the silent lyre!
    Dear sister of the wounded heart!
Could we but see her as she is,
    How we should long to hence depart!

Now as the days do come and go,
    She'll walk most softly by thy side;
With a holier, sweeter influence far,
    Than e'er before she died.

Died!—No, that is not the word!
    The pilgrim has not died!
But, having past the gates of fear,
    She worships on the other side.

LIGHTS AND SHADOWS.

The sweetest blossoms often spring,
   Where grows the fretting thorn,
And of our keenest agony,
   Is hope and patience born.

And tho' some tread the furnace floor,
   Till burns the heart to ashes,
Yet sometimes will a tear well up,
   And cool the burning lashes.

There's not an eye, however bright,
   But that a tear hath wet,
Nor rosy lip, tho' wreathed with smiles,
   But hideth some regret.

There is no heart, however pure,
   But needeth penitential prayer;
Nor yet a heart, so black with sin,
   But that a germ of good is there.

No prodigal doth ever roam
   From the dear homeward track,

But a home-sick feeling in the heart,
    In time will bring him back.

Nor one poor lamb doth stray,
    Far from the sheltering fold,
For a blest hand, which is unseen,
    The crimson cord doth hold.

There's not a bird, with wounded breast,
    Which sorely throbs and bleeds,
But is taught where grows the healing plant,
    Which our ignorance calls weeds.

There is no hope, however bright,
    But hath attendant fears,
And over each rejoicing day
    The night-fall weeps its tears.

Where'er the burnished sword of war
    Doth blood-ripe berries bear,
Its ripened seeds will spring and yield
    Freedom's rich harvest there.

No troubled year is ushered in,
    Which brings not blessed days,
In which the torn and bleeding feet
    May rest from weary ways.

There are tendrils in our human hearts
　　Which not even death can sever;
They will survive through light and shade,
　　Forever and forever.

There's life in death, and death in life,—
　　What if the mortal dies,
If from the ashes of the ruin
　　A deathless form arise?

O blessed realm! where no dark shade
　　Its gloomy form intrudes
To mar the joys of those who bask
　　In sweet beatitudes.

At set of sun, when all is o'er,
　　May Bethlehem's star shine bright;
Then to the shadows on life's dial
　　I'll say good-night — good-night.

IMMORTALITY.

"Being and thinking are identical."— HIGEL.

There is a sound philosophy,
   Simple, and yet 'tis strong;
It is, as the soul cannot cease to think,
   It must live on and on.

I think, by the yearning for my dead,
   That they somewhere wait for me,
Not where the mournful willows bend,
   Nor 'neath the dark yew tree.

O blessed sign in the inner heart!
   Bright cheering prophecy
Of immortality! a pledge
   Of our high destiny.

I think, by the sweet reunions here,
   Of loving souls and true,
That an eternal union waits,
   Which spirits claim as due.

I have thought by the calm, sweet, tranquil rest,
   Which ever follows pain,

That I shall rest, when the harvest's o'er,
   Amidst God's garnered grain.

In this decaying, clay-walled tent,
   This tottering temple of the soul,
The spirit waits, through calms and storms,
   The nearing of the goal.

And oft in the hush of the storm
   Are songs in the temple heard,
And fluttering, as of weary wings,
   Like those of a captive bird.

By the beaming glory of the sun,
   When the storm-cloud has passed by,
I think that a cloudless world awaits,
   Dear friend, for you and I.

By the aspirations of the soul,
   By the watchful eye and restless wing,
There must somewhere, in God's domain,
   Await for it eternal spring.

We know not where those mansions are,
   Where disembodied spirits go;
They're somewhere in our Father's house,
   Or Jesus would have told us so.

We know not how the soul is raised,
Nor what the body God will give;
But this we know, the Master sayeth,
Because he liveth, we shall live.

WHAT IS DEATH?—THERE IS NO DEATH.

'Tis but the loos'ning of the cord,
   The shattering of the golden bowl,—
The budding,— the transition state,—
   The expanding of the soul.

Talk not of death!—there is no death;
   Spirits immortal cannot die;
They but unfold their viewless wings,
   And soar on high.

What ye call death is a sweet friend,
   Who comes to unbar our prison gate;
Comes not alone, but shining ones
   Upon him wait.

He comes, the friend of human kind,—
   The white-winged messengers of peace;
He unlocks the fetters of the soul,
   And gives the sorrowing heart release.

What ye call death is not to sleep
   Unconciously beneath the sod,

Nor live beneath the burning wrath
   Of an avenging God.

'Tis sweet to breathe our lives away
   With him, who, hand in hand with time,
Is gathering sweet immortelles
   In every clime.

He comes into the sufferer's cot,
   Where long ago hath fled repose;
And where he plucks the piercing thorn,
   He plants the rose.

Here he takes a jewel rare,
   Which in heaven is needed most,
A father, or a mother dear,
   To swell the shining host.

As well might flowers mourn their decay,
   And grieve to mingle with the dust,
As we, that we must pass away,—
   In God we trust.

FLESH AND SPIRIT.

Spirit, thy loved companion tires
    Beneath the year's cold, heavy load;
Life's winter draweth on apace,
    The fires burn low along the road.

Ah, yes! thy loved companion tires,
    Around her fold thy heaven-fledged wing,
And with thy warmer, stronger love,
    Revive the fainting, drooping thing.

O tell her of the cool, green tent,
    Where waits the quiet, silent bed:
Where the pulseless heart no more will ache,
    And calm will rest the painless head.

Tho' oft she may have held thee back
    From high resolve and noble deed,
Yet could she see as thou dost see,
    For thy forgiveness she would plead.

The failing was not of the heart,
    But of the weary, throbbing head,

And the weight of the mortal vestment worn,
   Along the path compelled to tread.

Along that path thy kindly wing
   Hath often sheltered her from harm;
And, like the good Samaritan,
   Applied thy healing balm.

A strong supporting hope is thine,
   Which she may never know,—
When thou dost wing thy flight above,
   She to the silent dust must go.

The sacred union soon must end,
   Soon severed the mysterious tie,
Soon the pale messinger will come,
   And summons her to die.

The almond-tree begins to bloom,—
   A stranger, pale, at the gate doth knock;
So gather up thy strength to meet
   Nature's dissolving shock.

Fond recollection evermore
   Will to thy heavenly being cling,
And over her unconcious dust
   Thou'lt often poise thy loving wing.

HOUR OF ANGUISH.

Every pang which wrings a tear
   Lessens the heart-throbs for me here;
While every hour, by pain opprest,
   I'm nearing a world of painless rest.

One hour nearer to Him who cried
   In agony, just ere He died:
" If possible, remove this cup,"
   Yet, " thy will be done,"—"I'll drink it up."

Nearer to solving life's mysteries,
   Why some endure such agonies;
But O I shall learn why it was best,
   When I gain that home of perfect rest.

And I'm often thinking o'er and o'er,
   That I, with those who've gained that shore,
Shall learn from the unsealed book of life,
   Of things so dark in this world of strife.

Thus sang a sufferer, weak and pale,
   Whose feet drew near the shadowy vale:
"Though under the willow this form shall rest,
   My spirit to heaven will rise, so blest."

HOPE

Comes like the form of pity, bending
   O'er the image of despair;
Unto woe a radiance lending,
   Like a glorious sunbeam there.

How the heart would withering perish,
   But for this all-sustaining power,
Which ever doth its life-blood cherish,
   In the darkest, stormiest hour.

Ah, yes! that harp of thousand strings
   Would vibrate but with mournful tone;
And all its notes, sad murmurings,
   Would fill its chambers, dark and lone.

OUR FATHER WHO ART IN HEAVEN.

By every name which Thou art known
   In heathen or in christian lands,
On ice-bound coasts, in friged zones,
   Or on the fervid, glowing sands,—
They are dear, surpassing dear, to me,
Expressive of thy deity.

Jehovah!—How that august name,
   My being thrills with solomn awe;
That name the trembling prophet heard,
   When he received thy holy law;
With unveiled head, unsandaled feet,
Would I approach thy mercy-seat.

But there's a dearer, tenderer name,
   Which sweetly draws me to thy breast;
Nor height, nor depth, nor life, nor death,
   Hath power to make my soul unblest;
When I, in that dear name confide,
So peacefully the moments glide.

Our Father! thou who art in heaven!
   Thou whom the heavens cannot contain:

Thou deign'st to dwell in humble hearts,
    And in the contrite spirit reign;
Our Father! ever blessed name,
Now and forevermore the same.

As flow the rivers to the main,
    And as the flame ascendeth high,
My restless soul forevermore
    Seeketh its parent Deity.
Thou sacred name! I find thee here,
The name heaven's holy ones revere.

Blest name! thought after thought comes flowing
    on,
    Like a deep, surging sea,
Unsealing the deep founts of love
    From thine eternity,
Where pentecostal tongues of fire,
Would ever swell thy praises higher.

When thou dost call I'll answer thee,
    By this response,— this tender name,
"Our Father, who in heaven doth dwell,—
    To-day as yesterday the same."
E'en passing through the shades of death,
I'll chant it with my latest breath.

"HIS TENDER MERCIES ARE OVER ALL THE WORKS OF HIS HANDS"

Near as the heart which beats within our breast,
   Or as the breath on which our lives depend,
Yea, nearer still, in thee we move and breathe,
   Our Father, God, Creator, Lover, Friend.

Spontaneous as the curling smoke
   From smothered fire ascendeth high,
Or as the grass peeps out to meet the sun
   When early Spring is gently passing by,
Or as the rill from out the grassy lea
Flows ever onward to its parent sea.

So would our souls, unwarped by human creeds,
   Confiding, turn, and nestle in thy love,
As to the ark from the dark watery waste
   On gladsome wing returned the deluge-dove;
And we, our Father, we would cleave to thee,
Through life, in death, and in eternity.

Do we not see, tho' tenanted in clay,
   Our Father, when tired nature needs repose,

With kindly hand put out the light of day,
    As doth the mother round her curtains close,
That she her darlings peacefully may keep?
  So dost thou curtain our mysterious sleep.

And from our deep, unconscious sleep doth call,
    And with the call doth bring the light of day,
While with the light unnumbered blessings fall,
    Like Israel's manna all along our way,
To please the taste, the sight, the ear, the smell,
Thou ever doeth all things wise and well.

Far more than misers love their gold,
    Do we thy name, our Father, love;
For all thy attributes divine
    Which draws our heart above,
Most grateful at thy sacred feet,
May we thy praises oft repeat.

SYMPATHY.

When worn with suffering, pales the cheek,
    And red with weeping, dim the eye,
How often, with the sufferer meek,
    Hope gathers up itself to die!

Then, as the rainbow spans the cloud,
As heaven's sweet promise lights the shroud,
So does sympathy revive
Expiring hope, and bid her live.

'Tis hers to bind the aching head,
    To cool the burning, fevered brow,
And smooth the pillow of distress,
    When life is ebbing low.

Like an angel's silent tread
Around the sufferers dying bed,
She comes to cheer and soothe and bless,
And calm the anguish of distress.

O valued gift to mortals given,
Thy birth-place was the highest heaven;
Warm from the Father's bosom came,
And here on earth thou art the same.

HOPE IN AFFLICTION.

I have called thee Abba Father,
    I have said "Thou art my all;"
Now, o'erwhelmed with pain and sorrow,
    Let me on thy bosom fall.

Lamb of God! thou man of sorrow,
    Who the wine-press trod alone;
Thou hast felt the heart's deep anguish,
    Thou dost hear each plaintive moan.

O what am I?—Sad vigils keeping,
Other eyes than mine are weeping;
And other hearts, with anguish-pain,
Throb for the morning light in vain.

HEREAFTER.

O who will dwell hereafter
    In this loved home of mine?—
Whose hand will tend these lilies,
    And these morning-glories twine?

This dear-loved home of ours,
    Humble tho' it be,
To us it is a kingdom
    Ruled by him and me.

It teems with recollections
    Of pleasures which have been,
Of friends long since departed,
    Ne'er to return again.

There are sweet voices ling'ring
    In the hall and on the stair,
And when I fondly turn to greet them
    They are but forms of ambient air.

Then eagerly I lift the latch,
    And go softly down the walk,

Where I often seem to hear
　In sweet familiar talk,

The echo of a loved one's voice
　Which had scarcely died away;
But the grave's dark shadow rests
　Where he doth repose to-day.

And I shall one day go to him,—
　This is a joy to me;
And yet, my heart, bereft, doth moan,
　Like the shell beside the sea.

Heaven bless this home we love so well,
　Where we have joyed to meet
Those friends in the departed years
　Whose memory is so sweet.

May those who shall come after us
　Find on this quiet hearth
A genial home, a blest retreat.
　A joy-inspiring mirth.

God bless the hand that tends these flowers
　When I am here no more,
When like a migrant bird I've flown
　To seek a milder shore.

Oft when they pluck the lily,
  Or clasp the red heart of the rose,
May they bear them to some sufferer
  Where no sweet lily grows.

They are God's smiles;
  They lighten the grief we sometimes bear,—
I've known them lift a heart to heaven,
  In spite of all its care.

Then bear, O gently bear them,
  Where our country's heroes sleep:
Lay them calmly on their peaceful bed,
  And green their memory keep.

Bless all who make this house their home,—
  The hand which smooths the lawn,
The dimpled feet which brush the dew
  From off the grass at morn.

In every place within the gate
  Of this sweet, quiet nest,
In house, in garden, or on lawn,
  May they find comfort,—rest.

In this green arbor, where I've read
  Until the set of sun,
Then lingered till the stars came out
  In glory, one by one.

In this library, where in converse oft
  With the great, the good, and wise,
In hush'd communion, long I've sat
  In sweetest reveries.

By this consecrated window,
  Which looks towards the west,
Where beyond the saffron sunset bars,
  I've sometimes longed to rest.

Through the windows of this sanctum,
  The sun its glory pours,
Like a holy benediction
  Upon the winged hours.

The pictures on the sunlit walls
  Doth inspiration show,
While the anthracite within the grate
  Burns with a kindly glow.

THOUGHTS OF HEAVEN.

In that world where I am going,
    Whom will my companions be?
Will they be the ones who loved me,
    Ere they crossed the silent sea?

Who will be first to greet me there,
    Of all whom I have loved or known?—
Will heaven give back my cherished ones,
    My beautiful, my own?

Or will they have soared to mansions high,
    So deeply drank of love divine,
Attained to glories most transcendant,
    Needing no poor love of mine?

Will they be of kindred blood,
    Bound by consanguinity!
Or will souls be together drawn
    By chords of sweet affinity?

Those chords which kindred spirits feel,
    To vibrate at the slightest touch,

Kindling the noblest sympathies,
   Which angels love so much.

Will kindred hearts there meet and blend,
   From the great earth's remotest zone,
As waters of two distant seas
   Have met, and mingled into one?

Will all be pure and holy there,
   When first they enter in?—
Will heaven's gates forever bar
   Each sad effect of sin?

Will holiness invest the soul,
   With the immortal robe put on,
And the remembrance of earth's ills,
   Forever-more be gone?

May bliss not spring from memory,
   And yield a harvest of delight,
When earth's dark myst'ries are unveiled
   Before our wondering sight?

Will not each soul still holier grow,
   In that bright world above,
Forever drawing near its source
   Till merged in perfect love?

Shall I see Him, the Invisible,
  Who clothes himself in light,
Or, veiled between the cherubim,
  Will he never bless my sight?

Father, whatever else I find,
  However bright heaven's glories be,
Sound will be discord — sight but pain,—
  If I see not my Christ, and Thee!

WHO WILL WIND THE CLOCK?

There is silence in the cottage,—
   The doors stand open wide;
No cheerful ticking of the clock,—
   Some one has lately died.

Who will wind the clock?
   Who close the doors, and hide
The lonesome gloom, thick gathered there,
   Since she has died?

There's a solemn twilight in each room,
   A sorrow echoing tone;
The wind, which through the lattice comes,
   Comes with a hollow moan.

The flowers breathe in their fragrance
   Through the open garden door;
And with it comes an undertone,
   Which sigheth, nevermore.

How full of sad mementoes,—
   These rooms so dismal grown,—

So like a nest forsaken,
   When the mother-bird has flown.

Here's the picture of her own dear face,
   The robes which she did wear;
The chair in which she oft reclined,
   And a lock of auburn hair.

And here's her paper and her pen,
   The books she loved to read;
And there's the remnant of a loaf
   Which her pale hands did knead.

Who now will close the doors,
   When the evening hour comes on?
And who will light the lamps,
   Since the light of home is gone?

Make bright the fire on the hearth-stone,
   Light many lamps beside;
For the light of loving hearts went out
   The night on which she died.

Close round the lamps, O loving hearts!
   Nor let the hours seem long;
Let a calm peace of heaven be yours,
   Like her life's evening song.

She needeth none to wind the clock,
  Nor the pained head to bind;
For the bright hours of the better land
  Are measured by the mind.

ON SEEING GOD.

[The following lines were suggested by a conversation with a clerical friend, who thinks that we shall never see God, only as He manifests himself to us through Jesus Christ.]

What! no sweet vision of thy face divine
   When I have gained the everlasting hills;
When back to earth has gone the unconscious dust,
   With all its load of life-consuming ills?
Dear Lord, I feel within my being's core
That I shall see thee when this life is o'er.

Not through the windows of this house of clay,—
   So darkly dim, and cankered with earth-rust;
Not in the temple where we seek thy face,
   Shall we see thee, for whom our spirits thirst:
Since sin has darkened earth, no Eden-shade
Echoes thy footsteps through the dewy glade.

I see thy works,— the awe-inspiring heavens,
   Flashing with gems of ever-wondrous light:
The moon, serene, in majesty moves on,
   Adding her glory to the solemn night;

But O in heaven I must behold thy face,
Or heaven itself will seem a vacant place.
When I consider the high heavens,
   With all their hosts which thou hast made,
The vast infinitude of space,
   My heart sinks back almost afraid,
Permeated with thine awful power,
And immortality, — man's dower.

Lord, what am I?—A breathing mote,
   An atom in the balance laid:
What wonder that my human heart
   Doth sometimes feel afraid?
And yet I pine to see thy face,
In the pure heavens, thy dwelling-place.

And must I ne'er behold thee there?
   Must I in blindness worship thee?
And thou be visible to none
   Through thine eternity?
The faintest glance at the Divine
Would heaven's glories far outshine.

'Twould seem as if there were no God,
   If Love and Hope at last must end,
And I see not my soul's desire,
   My Father, God, and friend.
I crave not immortality,
If I my Lord may never see.

But if I ne'er may see thy face,
　　Only as I behold thee now,
O may I sometimes hear thy voice,
　　Saying, "Child, why weepest thou?"
Humbly I bow at thy behest,
My Father's voice must make me blest

TO DEATH.

Thou white-winged messenger of life and light,
Come in the silence of the solemn night;
Into my quiet chamber softly glide,
Nor wake the lov'd one sleeping by my side;
But from thy wings a balmy influence shed
To soothe his heart when I am with the dead,—
To wake him not 'till the last pang is o'er,
And I have entered where they die no more.

Pray send no sign—no word the day before,
Nor long stand waiting, knocking at the door,
But enter like some sweet, familiar friend,
And thy pale hand unto my soul extend.
Look calmly, gentle Death, when thou dost come,
Speak to my soul of its bright spirit-home,—
Just say, "The Master calls,"—I'll say " 'tis well,"
Then gently o'er me throw thy mystic spell.

DONE WITH EARTH.

Done with earth! done with earth!
   The spirit tries its wings;
Feebly dragging in the dust,
   It cleaves to earthly things.

Sympathies, long-nursed and tender,
   Hold the spirit here,
Where it hath pitch'd its clay-walled tent
   For many a happy year.

Unweaned love for earthly bliss
   Will not let the soul go free,
Hugs its fetters to the heart,
   Unknowing its high destiny.

Spirit! progress is the law
   By which thy powers unfold;
The casket must unclasp or break
   Which doth the jewel hold.

When past the shade which men call death,
   We shall not then be dead;

But as the chrysalis from its shell
    On joyous pinions sped.

Or gliding down the boundary stream,
    On its waves so gently toss'd,
Shall hear the voices of the past,
    Almost in the distance lost.

Eyeing worlds on worlds unnumbered,
    Thick as sands on ocean shore,
Where morning stars divinely hymning,
    Holy, holy, evermore.

Long, long eternities of twilight,
    Stretching onward to the goal,
E'er the full-orbed sun of glory
    Rises on the soul.

Ah, the twilight of that region
    Would eclipse our brightest day;
Would pale the suns of brightest systems
    By its faintest ray.

'Midst yon constellations bright,
    From all around, beneath, above,
Comes the thrilling anthem pealing,
    "God is love," "God is love."

Tall sons of light, heaven's vast arcana,
  Sound with trembling line,—
Eager inquiry droops her wing,
  'Midst wonders so divine.

There solving problems, deep and hoary,
  Ere our planet had its birth,—
Ranging countless worlds of glory,
  Done with earth! Done with earth!

www.ingramcontent.com/pod-product-compliance
Lightning Source LLC
Chambersburg PA
CBHW030317240426
43673CB00040B/1191